D0579371

SCHOOLS WITHOUT FAILURE

BOOKS BY WILLIAM GLASSER, M.D.

Mental Health or Mental Illness?: Psychiatry for Practical Action
Reality Therapy: A New Approach to Psychiatry
Schools Without Failure

SCHOOLS
WITHOUT
FAILURE

by William Glasser, M. D.

HARPER & ROW, PUBLISHERS

NEW YORK, EVANSTON, AND LONDON

1817

SCHOOLS WITHOUT FAILURE. Copyright © 1969 by William Glasser. Printed in the United States of America. All rights reserved. No part of this book may be used or reproduced in any manner whatsoever without written permission except in the case of brief quotations embodied in critical articles and reviews. For information address Harper & Row, Publishers, Incorporated, 49 East 33rd Street, New York, N.Y. 10016.

LIBRARY OF CONGRESS CATALOG CARD NUMBER: 68-28199

To my wife, Naomi,
and my children Joe, Alice, and Martin

Acknowledgments

For the third time, and more than ever, I must acknowledge the help of Robert Lloyd Glasser for the hundreds of hours he spent criticizing, questioning, commenting upon, and editing the manuscript.

As a newcomer to the field of education, I must thank the many professionals who have listened to me and encouraged me to continue. Among these friends are Donald O'Donnell, until recently principal of the Pershing Elementary School near Sacramento, now with the Palo Alto Schools. Mr. O'Donnell joined Palo Alto because of the interest and support shown by Dr. Harold T. Santee, superintendent of the Palo Alto schools, who has opened the doors of his schools to us.

Special mention must also be given to Dr. Robert J. Purdy, superintendent of elementary education of the Los Angeles city schools, who has given me the opportunity to work directly under him in an attempt to upgrade elementary education in the central area of Los Angeles.

For the past two years a large group of the Los Angeles city and county elementary administrators, counselors, and teachers have faithfully attended a class, helped me toward much of the thinking in this book, and made these ideas a part of their schools. While I cannot mention all these people, I must mention Douglas Naylor, principal of the 75th Street School in Los Angeles, and acknowledge his dedicated staff who have made me welcome in their classrooms.

viii   ACKNOWLEDGMENTS

Thanks also to Florence Itkin, principal of the Kenter Canyon Elementary School in Los Angeles, and Merle King, a member of her faculty, who contributed a major portion of one chapter in this book.

A final word of thanks goes to my hard-working, never-complaining secretary, Carol Kasday, and to my typists, Harriet Berkeley, Beatrice Tuby, Avis St. John, and Nancy Hollingsworth.

Contents

ix

Foreword

In this book, Dr. Glasser deals with the teaching process, basing his position upon his experiences and studies in a variety of school situations. He is not concerned here so much with subject matter as with people. He suggests that our typical schools are *designed for failure* and that those who succeed are usually those who can respond in ways prescribed by the teacher. Those who fail usually resent school, continue to have poor self-images, and too often become serious problems for the school and for society.

Schools Without Failure comes at a most opportune time, for we are all experiencing new problems affecting larger portions of our school-age population. While the magnitude of these problems, and indeed of the total education endeavor, is monumental, Dr. Glasser offers educators a way to bring relevance into the classroom. Problem solving, peer-group control of behavior, and development of attitudes toward and understandings of people of all races and socioeconomic levels are basic to Dr. Glasser's concept. Positive approaches by teachers and open-ended class discussions with no "right" answers, and greater opportunity for decision making by students create a stimulating environment for all. The self-image of the unsure is enhanced through participation and feelings of success.

Dr. Glasser's proposals for change do not replace subject matter but provide the opportunity for relevant use of subject matter as the vehicle for learning. These proposals are sound, simple, and, if properly understood and used by teachers, will go a long way toward reducing or eliminating the growing student militancy which feeds upon a program dominated by teacher and administrative fiat.

H. T. SANTEE, *Superintendent*
Palo Alto Unified School District
Palo Alto, California

Introduction

Too many students fail in school today. The rest are hampered by the intense pressure to succeed in schools where even many serious and qualified students do badly. Students fail in cities and suburbs, from elementary school to graduate school. They fail so consistently in the crowded, impoverished central city that many experts admit that here education is defeated, that whatever takes place in school is not education.

Although I believe we are far too complacent about school failure everywhere, no one will deny that education faces its most serious challenge in the center of our major cities. Confronted by overcrowded and dilapidated schools, children segregated by race, and many discouraged if not defeated teachers, we have a difficult task improving education here. In this book I emphasize central-city education because of the great need and because there, as nowhere else, people are open to making changes needed in all schools.

Much has been written on the difficulties of improving education in the central city. From personal experience, I believe that most people who write about these schools have not raised the critical issue. They have been so obsessed with the social, environmental, and cultural factors affecting students that they have not looked deeply enough into *the role education itself has played in causing students to fail, not only in the central city but in all schools*. It is the faults and shortcomings of the system itself that I wish to examine, and make suggestions to correct.

Certainly I am for improved living conditions and for integration, but these goals will be hard to reach unless we do much to improve education. Children can learn in Watts, and they can learn more in Beverly Hills. The main obstacle is our present educational philosophy, a philosophy of noninvolvement, nonrelevance, and limited emphasis on thinking. Education must move toward the opposite philosophy—*of involvement, relevance, and thinking*—or we will not solve the overwhelming problems of children who fail in school.

Schools Without Failure presents suggestions for making involvement, relevance, and thinking realities in our schools. All related to each other, these suggestions should be implemented as a whole. Separately they may have some merit, *but combined into a total program* they can provide a foundation upon which to build the schools our children need.

SCHOOLS WITHOUT FAILURE

CHAPTER ONE

The Problem of Failure

Because of the widespread interest in the ideas of Reality Therapy,* I conduct many day-long seminars for groups of people who work with problem children. First I discuss the theory of Reality Therapy; then I demonstrate the technique by interviewing a group of adolescents so that the audience can see in practice what I have described. If any reader of this book had been present at a recent demonstration in Portland, Oregon, and had not known that the audience was composed of social workers involved in helping delinquents, he would have been hard-pressed to understand the purpose of the interview. Listening to the attractive, well-groomed, poised, adolescent girls, anyone would have been favorably impressed with the comfort and ease with which they described their life before a large audience packed closely around them. The girls seemed so unlike the image the general public has of a delinquent. During their thoughtful and candid discussion of their problems, we became clearly aware that their attitude, an attitude distressing to both me and the audience, was that of resignation; *they believed they would have very little chance to succeed or to be happy* in the world as they saw it.

* A method of working with children and adults who have psychiatric problems, discussed in detail in my book *Reality Therapy* (Harper & Row, 1965).

These girls had all been in trouble with the law. Their juvenile offense was incorrigibility. Refusing to obey their parents, the school authorities, or the local juvenile curfew ordinances, they had, for example, stayed out all night, associated with people of whom their parents disapproved, cut school on many occasions, and dabbled in illegal drugs, alcohol, and sex. Although not hard-core delinquents, they had already been put into a local custodial institution; further trouble would lead them to the state reform school. Of the seven girls in the group, five firmly believed that they were failures in life and that they could not reverse this failure; the other two thought they might succeed in the school but had little confidence in success anywhere else. The five said that they would only go through the motions in school, that they had no hope of learning anything that would be valuable now or later in their lives. They realized that without a good education they were handicapped, but when I asked them whether they would work hard in school now that they recognized the gravity of their situation, they said they would only try hard enough to pass. Having accepted school failure, they would make no effort that might lead to success in school.

The girls also described their failure to make warm, constructive relationships with their families or their teachers; they even lacked warm feelings for each other, although they had lived together for several months. As they were resigned to school failure, so were they resigned to the lack of important human relationships. Although they were not happy in the institution they were living in, they predicted that they would do poorly at home, mostly because they had no confidence in their chances of succeeding in school. They readily admitted that most of their problems at home with their parents concerned school failure and their association with in-school or out-of-school failures. In the hour interview, I could not budge their conviction that all they could do now was take one day at a time and hope for the best. They had little interest in doing anything that might lead to a better future, or even in planning for one.

These girls did not have the classical sociological trappings of failure. They were attractive Caucasians from the middle class. Most were average or above in intelligence. Although some were from broken homes, each had at least one parent close to her who she believed loved her. Still, they were miserable; they had no confidence in themselves and they had no confidence for success in the future. Several admitted that if men came along who would marry them, they would accept, using marriage as a way out of a situation which seemed impossible for them to change by themselves. Nevertheless, they had little faith that a marriage would be successful. Having seen many broken marriages in her own family and among her friends, each doubted that her marriage would last. They hoped without conviction that it would, but they had no more understanding of how they might work toward a successful marriage than toward anything else successful. Since they had been removed from their homes and placed in an institution in which school was easy and their lives were strictly but, they admitted, pleasantly regulated, they were no longer even rebellious. Lackadaisical or apathetic might be a better description of their mood.

These girls are not unique. I have interviewed similar young people in many states from New York to California. There has sometimes been economic deprivation, sometimes racial discrimination, in rare instances physical impairment or mental retardation. But the primary explanation of their almost total lack of confidence in themselves and in their ability to improve their situation lies elsewhere. Poverty, while important, is not an overwhelming obstacle. Most children, and I now work with many children in poverty areas, don't really feel that they are poor. They are reasonably well-dressed, they have enough food, they have TV, and they have some of the material rewards that they know are available in our society. This may not be true everywhere, but it is mostly true in the Los Angeles central area I know best. Even for poorer children than those with whom I work or whom I have seen, poverty is not the sole or even the main cause of their hopelessness and resignation toward a future of failure. Similarly color, handicapping as it is to non-Caucasians in our society, is not a total obstacle. Combined with poverty, combined with a broken home and poor relationships with one's parents, and most of all, in my opinion, *combined with school failure,* the restricted opportunities that exist for nonwhites can be a very serious contribution to failure. *If school failure does not exist,* other handicaps can be more easily overcome.

If failing children, and the adults they become, were few, they would have little impact on our society; but they are not few. Congregating in the central section of any major city are increasing numbers of people whose common denominator is failure. This is not my definition of their condition, nor a sociologist's, a schoolteacher's, a policeman's, a probation officer's, nor a politician's; it is their definition of themselves. In a society where they are aware that many people are succeeding, they are failing. When pressed for a plan to do better, most will say that they must "work harder," but just what they are going to do is very vague in their minds. They are giving lip service to an old cliché.

Can this aura of failure be changed? Can we help these Portland girls with few social strikes against them develop goals, form better relationships with the important people in their lives, and start to experience success and gain confidence? Can we in addition find a solution for those who do have more social handicaps? I believe we can and I believe that the best solution, *a successful education,* can do much to overcome the problem of failure no matter what its social trappings. I do not accept the rationalization of failure commonly accepted today, that these young people are products of a social situation that precludes success. Blaming their failure upon their homes, their com-

THE PROBLEM OF FAILURE 5

munities, their culture, their background, their race, or their poverty is a dead end for two reasons: (1) it removes personal responsibility for failure, and (2) it does not recognize that school success is potentially open to all young people. If students can gain enough responsibility to work hard in school, and if the built-in barriers to success are removed from all schools, many of the detrimental conditions can be overcome.

As a psychiatrist, I have worked many years with people who are failing. I have struggled with them as they try to find the way to a more successful life. As I became involved with them, I have shared their pains and misfortunes and fought against their rationalizations. From these struggles I have discovered an important fact: regardless of how many failures a person has had in his past, regardless of his background, his culture, his color, or his economic level, *he will not succeed in general until he can in some way first experience success in one important part of his life.* Given the first success to build upon, the negative factors, the ones emphasized by the sociologists, mean little.

From this observation, gained from eleven years of helping delinquent girls in a reform school,* my work has taken me to the public schools. I believe that if a child, no matter what his background, can succeed in school, he has an excellent chance for success in life. If he fails at any stage of his educational career—elementary school, junior high, high school, or college—his chances for success in life are greatly diminished.

From a community standpoint, we will never be able to do much to correct the serious problems in homes and families. Although broken homes will always have a bad effect upon the children they send to school, the schools need not therefore give up. As a nation, however, we can and we must rid ourselves of racial discrimination and increase opportunities for employment, particularly meaningful employment in which the

* See *Reality Therapy,* Chapters 1 and 3.

worker feels that he is doing a good, worthwhile job. Racial discrimination and lack of job opportunities presently contribute markedly to the failure we see in our society. However, even if we do correct these grave deficiencies, if we do not simultaneously examine education and find out how to graduate more well-educated and successful students, much of what else we do will be wasted.

We must develop schools where children succeed, not only in our wealthy suburbs, but in all parts of our cities, from upper-middle-class neighborhoods down through the poverty-stricken central city.* It is the responsibility of each individual child to work to succeed in the world, to rise above the handicaps that surround him; equally it is the responsibility of the society to provide a school system in which success is not only possible, but probable. Too much of our present educational system emphasizes failure and too many children who attend school are failing. *Unless we can provide schools where children, through a reasonable use of their capacities, can succeed, we will do little to solve the major problems of our country.* We will have more social disturbances, more people who need to be kept in jails, prisons, and mental hospitals, more people who need social workers to take care of their lives because they feel they cannot succeed in this society and are no longer willing to try. It is with the crucial importance of the school system in mind that I have moved from the traditional but limited psychiatric practice of working in prisons, mental hospitals, and clinics into working with children and teachers in school to see whether the concepts of Reality Therapy, especially involvement and responsibility, applied to the public schools, can work as well there as in reform schools and mental hospitals.

No one is more aware of the problems of failing children

---

* Although I have no experience working in rural schools, I am sure that many of them need the same program that I recommend for urban and suburban schools.

than those who work in the schools. Almost every teacher and administrator I have spoken to in the past several years has been disturbed, puzzled, and in many cases disheartened over the increasing numbers of children who seem to be totally recalcitrant to the school process. They are rebellious, they do not read, they are unmotivated, they are withdrawn, they are apathetic. They seem to be impossible to educate. Faced with these problem children, those who work in the schools have tried and continue to try many new approaches. They expect that with my experience in working with children who are rebellious, nonconforming, withdrawn, and apathetic, I will be able to contribute some effective procedures to the schools. Coming from a discipline outside the schools, I think I can see some of the problems more clearly than those who are much closer. Perhaps my major contribution up to this time has been that I see that *the major problem of the schools is a problem of failure.* Therefore, ways must be discovered so that more children can succeed. To discover these ways, we must examine the reasons why children are failing and develop an educational philosophy that leads to an atmosphere in which success is much more possible. *We must implement this philosophy in the classroom where it counts,* not merely pay lip service to it in schools of education, books, or conferences.

Regardless of the reasons for failure, *any recommendations for change must fall within the existing framework of the schools.* That is, it will do no good to recommend as the *only* solution that we hire many more people, that we build better buildings, that we increase the training of teachers, that we hire more specialists, or that we do anything that will greatly increase the school budget. We will continue to have large classes and few specialists in the schools. I do not say that more personnel, better teacher training, smaller classes, and other educational advantages will not help, nor am I opposed to these changes. Far from it; but what I recommend in this book is applicable to the existing conditions in the schools, conditions that I believe can be greatly improved with little additional expense.

I soon discovered that any attempt by the schools to use specialists to work with individual children, or even with small groups of children, would not dent the failure problem that the schools face. Even if each school had its own psychiatrist, if he worked within the traditional framework of seeing children outside of class, individually or in small groups, nothing would change. The traditional psychiatric-sociologic approach is ineffective because it assumes that school problems are almost entirely a reflection of individual personal problems, poor home environment, poverty, and racial discrimination. In contrast, it is apparent to me and to most of the educators I work with that, although external environmental conditions are bad for many children, *there are factors inherent within the education system itself that not only cause many school problems but that accentuate the problems a child may bring to school.*

In asking for my help, the schools expected that I would follow the traditional approach to problems, one used in every part of our society today. This approach is: don't investigate the part played by the system in causing difficulties; instead, when difficulties arise, separate those in trouble from the system and treat them by specialists. Separation and treatment by specialists, a concept that guides almost all juvenile correctional and mental health programs in the United States today, has made a serious intrusion into the schools. The concept is somewhat erroneous for juvenile offenders and mental patients, but right or wrong, it makes little difference to the average man or to the country as a whole. For the schools, whose problems dwarf the problems of mental health or juvenile correction in immediacy, concern to the nation, and the numbers of people involved, the concept of separation and treatment by specialists is disastrous. Rather than follow the inadequate, traditional procedure that we too often use unsuccessfully with prisoners and mental patients, we must keep children with educational problems in heterogeneous schools* and, with few exceptions, heterogeneous classrooms. We must and we can find ways to help them gain enough from regular schools and regular classes so that they need not be removed from them for individual and group treatment by specialists. The specialists in the schools—counselors, psychologists, remedial instructors—should help the teacher in the classroom cope with the problems she has, both disciplinary and educational. They should examine in what ways classroom education can be improved and they should implement their ideas in the regular classes *in cooperation* with the classroom teachers. Children may be removed on occasion for special help, but that help should be directed toward better functioning in the heterogeneous classroom.

Although educational failure is widespread in all communities, it exists in epidemic proportions in the poor neighborhoods of any city. My experience in the central city of Los Angeles reveals that 75 percent of the children do not achieve a satisfactory elementary education. That is, three out of every four children who leave elementary school have not achieved the standard sixth-grade skills in reading and arithmetic. These children will not develop these skills in junior and senior high. Rather, their numbers will grow as the work gets harder and the system less personal. For practical purposes, education in the central city is a failure, producing thousands of young people cut off from any but the most menial employment.† Almost the only way to succeed in America today is to begin with a valid education certified by a valid diploma. Even a nonacademic certificate (that is, a diploma gained by regular attendance and good conduct, although its holder can barely

---

* Heterogeneous schools are schools in which the serious behavioral and educational problems are kept in the school, not separated and sent elsewhere.

†Although employment is not the only goal of an education (in fact, it is probably emphasized far out of proportion to its absolute worth), without a chance to work at some meaningful job, few of the other benefits of education are realized.

read or write) is much better than nothing at all. Few students, however, can go through school with attendance as their major mark of success. In the central city only a small minority hold academic diplomas; a few more hold nonacademic certificates. Those who fail provide a reservoir of people to populate our jails, mental hospitals, and welfare rolls, people who live their lives in misery and failure, whose only stepping stone to success, an education, is no longer attainable. An increasing burden on the remainder of society, these educational failures are rarely patched up by welfare workers, psychologists, psychiatrists, prisons, or mental hospitals. Convinced of their failure, many live their lives in resignation or sometimes, as we see more recently, in rebellion against the system that has not provided them, from their standpoint, with a chance to succeed.

We will never succeed in patching people up. We must get them responsibly involved from early childhood in an educational system in which they can *succeed enough* to function successfully in our society. If we are to eliminate black ghettos, racial discrimination, and unequal opportunity, we must have young people who gain valid diplomas and who then go out into a society with more opportunity than ever for people of all races to succeed *if they have the educational credentials.* Everywhere in Southern California we see Negroes and Mexican Americans in jobs for which in the past their applications would have been rejected. For the first time (in 1967) I have flown on three major airlines and seen Negro stewardesses! I don't claim that this observation has sweeping significance, but it is tangible indication of progress in an occupation where discrimination ruled too long.

Although educational practice may be deficient in approximately the same way in different neighborhoods, it will have its worst effect on children from poor homes. The report *Equality of Educational Opportunity,* commonly called the Coleman Report, states that, "It is for the most disadvantaged children that improvements in school quality will make the most difference in achievement." Where children come from homes in which failure is a part of the home and neighborhood environment, deficient education leads to no motivation or to anti-motivation. Without motivation, or in a battle against an education which makes no sense to them, they fail in school, usually locking themselves into failure for life. In wealthier neighborhoods, where homes are successful and the environment strongly motivates toward success, deficient education does not so often lead to failure. Most children learn to play the testing, memorizing, nonthinking games enough to gain a valid diploma, the main ticket to opportunity in life. Many do not, however; they present serious problems in suburbia, and most sensitive suburban educators are far from complacent about what is happening in their schools.

Although we have much to learn about improving education, some ideas are here and available, but not yet used. Education right now can be upgraded enough to reduce failures through an investment small compared to that of total environmental approaches, yet we are dragging our feet because some of the basic improvements that must be made *break with tradition*. Today we have no choice but to make this break. First we must examine the deficiencies in education itself that lead to school failure, then set a course which will correct them. If we cannot do so, we will have cut off the major, perhaps the only, escape route from our present descent into increasing social disorganization.

CHAPTER TWO

Reality Therapy and Failure

In Chapter 1, great stress was laid upon failure. There appear to be many kinds of failure, of which school failure is usually considered only one. *This appearance is misleading;* there are not many kinds of failure. According to the concepts of Reality Therapy, described in my previous book, there are two kinds of failure; but even these two, failure to love and failure to achieve self-worth, are so closely interrelated that it is difficult and probably artificial to separate them. (Although in this chapter we shall discuss failure of young children, the principles hold for all ages.)

To see that failure is far more singular than plural and to put it into a context that can be dealt with adequately by the schools, we must examine (here slightly differently from the way it was done in my previous book) the basic needs of people. In *Reality Therapy,* the basic needs are described as the need for love and the need for self-worth. A person must learn to give and receive love; he must find someone in the world to love and someone in the world who loves him, many people, if possible, but at the minimum one person he loves and one person who loves him. If a person succeeds in giving and receiving love, and can do so with some consistency throughout his life, he is to some degree a success. Ordinarily, one thinks that the need for love will be fulfilled in the home rather than in the school or other outside institutions. Closer examination, however, shows this belief to be false. Teachers are overwhelmed with children who need affection, but at present they do not know how to react to the obvious need for love of many of their students. Children who need affection desperately, not only from teachers but from each other, have little opportunity to gain that affection in school. To say that helping to fulfill the need for love is not a school function is tantamount to saying that children who don't succeed in giving and receiving desperately needed affection at home or in their community (outside of school) will have little chance to do so. Having failed to learn to love as a child, an adult is in a poor position ever to learn love. How the schools can and should get involved to help children fulfill their need for love will be discussed in detail later in this book.

The schools are much more directly concerned with the second basic need, the need to feel worthwhile. Knowledge and the ability to think are required to achieve worthwhileness. If a child goes to school and fails to gain knowledge, to learn to think and to learn to solve problems, it is unlikely that his family or his environment will correct this failure. In addition, in learning to think and to solve problems, essential to attaining a feeling of self-worth, a child may gain enough self-confidence to learn to give and receive love. At least he has a greater chance for fulfilling his need for love because, when he feels worthwhile, he can tolerate some rejection that may occur when he tries to love. A person who is loved and who learns to give love also has some chance of succeeding in the world; from love he develops motivation to succeed and to feel worthwhile. If he does not learn, however, to give love, but only receives it, he will often fail, as exemplified by the spoiled, pampered, and over-protected child who wonders why the world does not respond to him as did his unwise parents.

Love and self-worth are so intertwined that they may properly be related through the use of the term *identity*. Thus we may say that the single basic need that people have is the requirement for an identity: the belief that we are someone in distinction to others, and that the someone is important and worthwhile. Then *love and self-worth may be considered the two pathways* that mankind has discovered lead to a successful identity. People able to develop a successful identity are those who have learned to find their way through the two pathways of love and self-worth, the latter dependent upon knowledge and the ability to solve the problems of life successfully.

For most children only two places exist where they can gain a successful identity and learn to follow the essential pathways. These places are the home and the school. As stated previously, *if* the home is successful, the child may succeed despite the school, but that is too big an *if* to rely upon. We must ensure that the child's major experience in growing up, the most constant and important factor in his life, school, provides within it the two necessary pathways: a chance to give and receive love and a chance to become educated and therefore worthwhile.

In the context of school, love can best be thought of as social responsibility. When children do not learn to be responsible for each other, to care for each other, and to help each other, *not only for the sake of others but for their own sake,* love becomes a weak and limited concept. Teachers and children need not love each other in a narrow family or even narrower romantic sense, but they must learn to care enough to help one another with the many social and educational problems of school. Education for social responsibility should be a part of every school program. If it is not, many children will not gain successful identities. Even a relatively warm and successful home will not usually counterbalance school failure, although children from such homes rarely fail. Our society cannot depend upon the home to correct failure in school. Therefore the schools must provide the pathways for each child to fulfill his basic need for a successful identity.

Inability to gain a success identity does not mean that a person will have *no* identity. Very few people lead a life with no real knowledge of who they are. They are a few of the long-term patients at any mental hospital and some of the characters and winos who inhabit skid rows, county jails, and "work farms" of any large city. These few people, however, are no great burden on society. In contrast, the many people who do not gain a success identity and end up with a failure identity are presenting us with dramatic and seemingly insuperable problems.

Although it would also seem logical to have many people with mixed identity, partly failing and partly succeeding, in my experience this does not occur. A person functions at any time feeling either that he is a success and enjoying the psychological comforts of success or that he is a failure and desperately trying to avoid the attendant psychological discomforts. Rarely does he feel both strongly; one usually dominates the other. Therefore, if a person cannot develop an identity through the two pathways of love and self-worth, he attempts to do so through two other pathways, delinquency and withdrawal. Delinquency and withdrawal do lead to an identity, a failure identity. The more they are used, the more solid the failure identity becomes. Those who are failing must learn, in school if nowhere else, what seems to them to be impossible: that open to them are the alternate pathways of love and self-worth that can lead to a success identity. Further, they must gain the confidence to take the better pathways.

A child failing at home, feeling unwanted, feeling little love and self-worth, is in a desperate position. He still must maintain an identity; it is built into his system that he must create a feeling of who he is. If he cannot do so at home, he may try to do so in the community by joining others who have small sense of identity. Trying in their own way to gain some sense of self-worth and the feeling that they care for someone, they are almost always unsuccessful. Disregard of the law often leads to arrest. (In a twisted way they may thus find someone who cares, a probation officer if no one else.) Because they can't fulfill their needs adequately, because they can't find love and self-worth, they become angry and frustrated, reacting against a society that they think is depriving them of a chance to fulfill their needs. Becoming hostile and aggressive, they try to gain their needs forcefully. If they are frustrated in these unsuccessful attempts, or if they are afraid to take the delinquent path, they suffer and withdraw.

They suffer and withdraw because they can't find the successful pathways to a success identity. We wrongly label variations of this suffering and withdrawal "mental illness." Such people are not ill; nothing has happened to them that they can't remedy themselves. Illness implies that a person has been attacked by a bacteria, toxin, or chemical imbalance over which he has no control. In helping children, we must work to make them understand that *they are responsible* for fulfilling their needs, for behaving so that they can gain a successful identity. No one can do it for them. If they continue to choose pathways that lead to failure, that diminish their self-worth, that are without love, they will continue to suffer and continue to react with delinquency or withdrawal. Although this book is highly critical of schools for the roadblocks they put in the path of students attempting to achieve a successful identity, I do not wish to diminish the responsibility of each student to work hard for his education. Without hard work and personal discipline, students will fail no matter how much we improve schools.

When children can't fulfill their needs at home, they must do so at school. To begin to be successful, children must receive at school what they lack: a good relationship with other people, both children and adults. A child or adult cannot gain a success identity and fulfill his needs through the established pathways because he is lonely. While we may call him by various euphemisms such as "culturally deprived," "disadvantaged," "alienated," "isolated," or even the word I prefer, "uninvolved," his basic problem is that within his family and his community he has not found people to whom he can successfully relate. As a child, therefore, his only hope is to find these people in school. If he continues to be lonely he will not fulfill his need for identity; the pathway of love and the pathway of self-worth, which require worthwhileness in the eyes of others, are closed to him.

Thus, those who fail in our society are lonely. In their loneliness they grope for identity, but to the lonely the pathways to success are closed; only anger, frustration, suffering, and withdrawal—a failure identity—are open. Successful people relate successfully to others; failures associate somewhat with each other but still complain that they are often lonely and isolated. The failure of disadvantaged people, related as it may be to inadequate home life, economic deprivation, or race, stems from loneliness—sometimes loneliness in their own homes, almost always loneliness in the greater community, *and too often loneliness in school.* The schools have not faced the problem of failure caused by loneliness; many have refused to admit that it is a problem or, if they admit it, they say it is not their problem. A suggested way for the schools to reduce loneliness and its consequent failure is the use of classroom meetings, a method described fully later in the book.

The schools are in a unique position to eliminate or at least greatly reduce the loneliness of their children. They are preponderantly staffed by warm, successful people who care greatly for children, but who have become disillusioned in expressing affection by the lack of provision for it in the school program. Schools also can offer students the basic ingredients of self-worth: knowledge and thinking. School can be organized to stimulate children to solve problems, both academic and social. A purpose of this book is to show how schools can get involved with children, can break the loneliness that too many children bring to school, a loneliness that leads to failure.

With individuals in the psychiatric office, at the Ventura School,* or anywhere that Reality Therapy is practiced, loneliness is overcome by the therapist, a successful person, becoming involved with the lonely person. When Reality Therapy is practiced in large groups, however, the therapist must not only become personally involved with many in the group, but he must also stand as an example of responsible involvement so that members of the group can learn to become involved with each other and begin to function as a working, problem-solving group. Unfortunately involvement, vital to success, hardly exists in our schools.

Where traditional psychiatry teaches that the therapist must stay uninvolved and aloof emotionally from the lonely patient, Reality Therapy states that there must be a real, warm, positive involvement. Probably drawing on the teachings of traditional psychiatry, many traditional educators wrongly believe that teachers should not become emotionally involved with their pupils. They give lack of motivation as the reason that so many children fail in school, although they cannot explain this widespread lack of motivation. Their attempts to apply external pressure upon students to try to motivate them generally fail. In contrast, Reality Therapy does not concern itself directly with motivation. We don't attempt direct motivation because we know that it can be produced only with a "gun" or some other forceful method. But guns, force, threats, shame, or punishment are historically poor motivators and work (if we continue the gun example) only as long as they are pointed and as long as the person is afraid. If he loses his fear, or if the gun is put down, the motivation ceases.

Traditional psychiatry does not use a gun because it assumes that every patient has a built-in motivation that can be liberated through the patient's gaining insight, an incorrect concept described in my previous book. The schools assume built-in

* A custodial institution for the most delinquent girls in California, where the author worked for eleven years. See *Reality Therapy*.

motivation, but when it does not occur, they attempt to motivate children with methods analogous to using a gun. Although guns have never worked, the schools, struggling to solve their problems, resort to using bigger and bigger guns—more restrictions and rules, more threats and punishments. Reality Therapy says that teachers and students must become involved; that when students are involved with responsible teachers, people who themselves have a success identity and can fulfill their needs, the students are then in a position to fulfill their own needs.

Students are responsible for fulfilling their needs, they are responsible for their behavior, they are not mentally ill but are making bad choices when their behavior is deviant; nevertheless, they can't make better choices, more responsible choices, unless they are strongly and emotionally involved with those who can. In education, involvement may start with one person, be he teacher, counselor, or administrator, or it may start with groups of children or even with a whole class. Both in psychiatry and in school, teachers and therapists too often stand aloof from children; they do not get emotionally involved; they are not warm, personal and interested; they do not reveal themselves as human beings so that the children can identify with them. Thus they fail to alleviate the loneliness of the many children who need human warmth so desperately. Only in a school where teacher and student are involved with each other and equally involved with the curriculum through thinking and problem solving does education flourish—an education that prepares students to live successfully in the world.

To become involved we must understand that although a child has failed in the past, he can succeed in the present if the necessary teacher-pupil involvement concerns the problems of the present. A failing child will continue to fail if the teachers who work with him remind him of his failure. Failure breeds failure; to break the cycle of failure, we must work in the present and realize that a person who has failed all his life can succeed if he can become involved with a responsible person. Much of the record-keeping and anecdotal material transferred from teacher to teacher acts as a millstone of failure around the neck of the pupil. A student judged and found guilty from his record may never succeed, until he can realize that from now on he will not be damned for what he has done in the past. Whether we work in therapy or in the schools, we must work with the present failure, utilizing the past only as it relates to past success or to the possibility of present success. The belief that a child cannot be helped until we understand his past is wrong. Most often an understanding of the past really means understanding past failures. The records and case histories of students who fail devote themselves primarily to past failures. The only worthwhile information, however, to be gleaned from the past concerns the child's successes; this knowledge can be used to help him in the present. The past of people who fail is filled with failures. It is useless to work with failure because the teacher (or the therapist) and the child become deeply involved with failure; believing that his failure is an important part of his relationship to the teacher, the child continues to fail. By ignoring the past failure, we encourage the child to change his present behavior; his past is not important to us. To summarize, we do work with failing students, but we limit our work to what the child is doing now and his present attempts to succeed.

Following the concepts of Reality Therapy, we must not be misled by emotion. *People who fail fall back upon emotion to direct their behavior;* people who succeed rely upon reason and logic. Of course, the result of any behavior is emotion, with successful behavior producing pleasant emotions in contrast to the suffering of unsuccessful people. In addition, therefore, to developing a warm, positive, personal involvement with students and working with them in the present, we must deal with their *behavior* because only their behavior can be changed. One cannot change emotion directly. *Emotion is the result of be-*

havior, but it is the behavior and the behavior alone that can be improved. When behavior is improved, it leads to good feelings that in turn snowball toward better behavior. Although our involvement must not ignore feelings, when we are trying to change behavior we must always relate feelings to behavior. When a person changes his behavior and feels better, our involvement with him deepens. Too often in the past, when people responded to his feelings and ignored his behavior in an attempt to help him feel better, he continued to fail and in the end suffered more.

Assuming that we learn to work with children by becoming personally involved and dealing with their present behavior, we must help them to change their behavior toward more success. To help a presently failing child to succeed, *we must get him to make a value judgment about what he is now doing that is contributing to his failure.* If he doesn't believe that what he is doing is contributing to his failure, if he believes his behavior is all right, no one can change the child now. He must then suffer the consequences of his refusal to change his behavior. *Neither school nor therapist should attempt to manipulate the world so that the child does not suffer the reasonable consequences of his behavior.* But we should not give up; accepting failure is not a reasonable consequence. No matter how often he fails, he should again and again be asked for a value judgment until he begins to doubt that what he is defending is really the best for him.

If a child misbehaves in class, the teacher must ask, "What are you doing?" If she is warm and personal, if she deals with the present and does not throw the child's past misdeeds in his face, he will almost always reply honestly and tell what he is doing. The teacher must then ask, in words appropriate to the age of the child and to the situation, whether his behavior is helping him, her, the class, or the school. If the child says, "No, what I am doing is not helping," the teacher must then ask the child what he could do that is different. This is exactly the opposite of what happens in almost all schools and homes when a child misbehaves. Ordinarily, the teacher or parent tells the child that he is doing wrong and that if he doesn't change he'll be punished. This traditional but ineffective approach removes the responsibility for his bad behavior from the child. The teacher makes the judgment and enforces the punishment; the child has little responsibility for what happens.

In Reality Therapy, the child is asked to select a better course of behavior. If he doesn't know a better course, the teacher should suggest some alternatives and thus help the child plan a better course of behavior. Irresponsible children usually don't know how to behave better. They depend upon us to help them figure out a better way, help them make a plan. For example, if a child talks continually and interrupts the class, the teacher might, with the child, work out a new seating arrangement in which the child is away from children who excite him so that he loses control. This simple plan carried out in cooperation with the child helps him to be quiet. *The child has the responsibility, he makes the decision from his own evaluation, and thus he learns responsibility—something to which we give lip service but which we do not teach in school.* We teach thoughtless conformity to school rules and call the conforming child "responsible." Although he may be conforming, he is not necessarily responsible. Responsibility is learned only by evaluating the situation and choosing a path that a person thinks will be more helpful to himself and to others. Given an opportunity to learn this from kindergarten onward, children can become responsible and socially aware; we will then need fewer rules and punishments.

It is not enough, however, for the child to make a value judgment; he must choose a better way and commit himself to his choice. It is from commitment that we gain maturity and worthwhileness. It is from commitment that we gain understanding of real love. *We must teach children commitment.* We cannot be like Mark Twain when he explained that it was easy to stop smoking: he had done it a thousand times. A person must make a commitment based upon the judgment that smoking is harmful. Then and only then will he stop smoking—or stop disturbing the school and start learning.

Finally, and this is the keystone of Reality Therapy, when a child makes a value judgment and a commitment to change his behavior, no excuse is acceptable for not following through. This is discipline. Society and the schools mainly use punishment, and punishment doesn't work. Although with discipline the child suffers the painful consequences of his misbehavior, no attempt is made to cause excess pain or be punitive. A child may be excluded from class or school if he misbehaves, but not for an arbitrary time, only until he proposes a plan to return and states his commitment to follow his plan.

In punishment, pain follows an act that someone else disapproves of, and the someone else usually provides the pain; with discipline, in contrast, the pain is a natural and realistic consequence of a person's behavior. Unlike punishment, discipline is rarely arbitrary; it asks only that a student evaluate his behavior and commit himself to a better course. Discipline also requires the involvement of an important person during the evaluation and commitment. For discipline to be successful, the important person—the teacher—must under no circumstances accept any excuse for a commitment not being fulfilled. If she takes an excuse, she breaks the involvement because the student then knows she really doesn't care. Involvement ceases because a person who makes a commitment and is then allowed to excuse himself out of it knows that he is being harmed; he cannot continue to be involved with anyone who lets him harm himself. *Teachers who care accept no excuses.* A perfect example showing the teacher who cares is Annie Sullivan's work with the handicapped Helen Keller, an example explained in *Reality Therapy.*

Today increasing numbers of students fail to gain a successful identity and react illogically and emotionally to their failure.

Because they are lonely, they need involvement with educators who are warm and personal and who will work with their behavior in the present. They need teachers who will encourage them to make a value judgment of their behavior rather than preach or dictate; teachers who will help them plan better behavior and who will expect a commitment from the students that they will do what they have planned. They need teachers who will not excuse them when they fail their commitments, but who will work with them again and again as they commit and recommit until they finally learn to fulfill a commitment. When they *learn* to do so, they are no longer lonely; they gain maturity, respect, love, and a successful identity.

CHAPTER THREE

The Impact of School

Schools fail to teach children to gain and to maintain a successful identity through the need pathways of social responsibility
and self-worth. Discussed extensively in later chapters, social
responsibility (love in the school situation) is mentioned only
briefly here. The role of the school in teaching children self-
worth, in giving them the knowledge and tools necessary to
succeed in our society, concerns us now. Having been asked to
work with children who had failure identities as shown by their
behavioral problems and educational failure, I immediately saw
the difficulty of trying to help them. The task was difficult,
perhaps impossible, because the current philosophy of education, which emphasizes failure, prevents the students from developing a feeling of self-worth. To understand what has happened, let us examine the child before he comes to school and
follow him through his first years of formal education.

Education begins at birth and continues all our lives. School,
especially elementary school, was developed to standardize education during the early years. In the few years before school, a
child learns much about life. Considering that he is helpless at
birth, he is a reasonably competent individual when he enters
kindergarten. He has learned much about the world and he
usually feels that he can cope with it; whatever his environ-

ment, he is optimistic about his future. Very few children come to school failures, none come labeled failures; *it is school and school alone which pins the label of failure on children.* Most of them have a success identity, regardless of their homes or environments. In school they expect to achieve recognition and, with the faith of the young, they hope also to gain the love and respect of their teachers and classmates. The shattering of this optimistic outlook is the most serious problem of the elementary schools. Whatever their background, children come to school highly receptive to learning.* If they then fail to continue to learn at their rapid preschool rate, we may if we wish blame it on their families, their environment, or their poverty, but we would be much wiser to blame it on their experience in school. Considering the great emphasis today upon school and education, and recognizing that for most small children school is the only part of their world that exists primarily for them, we can see that school must be and is an extremely important part of their lives. If school is failing to do the job that it should do, we should not look for environmental scapegoats, we should improve the school. Many educators who work with children from "disadvantaged backgrounds" believe that *the first years of school are critical for success or failure.* I agree completely, *not only for deprived children but for all children.*

A child who has functioned satisfactorily for five years is confident that he will continue to do so in school. In the experience of many of us working in the schools, this confidence may wane but will still remain effective for about five more years, regardless of how inadequate his school experience is. If, however, the child experiences failure in school during these five years (from ages five to ten), by the age of ten his confidence will be shattered, his motivation will be destroyed, and he will have begun to identify with failure. Convinced that he is unable to fulfill

---

* Dr. Elliot Shapiro, principal of P.S. 119, an elementary school in a poverty area of Harlem in New York City, found this to be true. His work is movingly described in *Our Children Are Dying*, by Nat Hentoff, Viking, 1966.

his needs through the logical use of his brain, he will return to behavior directed by his emotions, behavior that he had learned to avoid when he was successful in the past. He will abandon the pathways of love and self-worth and grope blindly toward what seem to him to be the only paths left open, those of delinquency and withdrawal. Although success in school is still possible, with each succeeding year it becomes more difficult and more unlikely. The number who try again toward the end of high school, in junior college, in night school, or after service in the armed forces is not large enough to make much difference.

The five-hundred girl Ventura School, with almost as many highly trained psychological personnel as the entire Los Angeles school system, with one staff member for every two girls, with an expenditure of $18 a day per girl (without considering the $10 million plant investment) , is able to rehabilitate only 60 to 70 percent of its girls. Most have had at least ten years of solid failure; few can remember any satisfactory school experience. If these girls had had an elementary school experience similar to the total experience they gain at Ventura, many more would have succeeded, much suffering would have been avoided, and many of these bright, articulate girls could have contributed to, rather than burdened, society.

The critical years are between ages five and ten. Failure, which should be prevented throughout school, is most easily prevented at this time. When failure does occur, it can usually be corrected during these five years within the elementary school classrooms by teaching and educational procedures that lead to fulfillment of the child's basic needs. The age beyond which failure is difficult to reverse may be higher or lower than ten for any one child, depending upon the community he comes from, the strength of his family, and his own genetic resources; regardless of these variations, however, it is amazing to me how constant this age seems to be. Before age ten, a good school experience can help him succeed. After age ten, it takes more than a good school experience, and, unfortunately, shortly after age ten he is thrust into junior and senior high situations where he has much less chance for a corrective educational experience. Therefore, although children can be helped at any school level, the major effort should be in the elementary school.

Much has been written recently about the need to prepare children, especially those from poor families, for school. It is said that these children are nonverbal, that their nonintellectual environments cause poor learning patterns, and that they need to be given preschooling to bring them to the level at which children from more intellectual environments start school. "Operation Head Start" is the name given to the major program of such preschooling. In Operation Head Start, much of what I will advocate later in this book is applied successfully. Head Start children do enter school with better intellectual preparation than other children from the same neighborhood. Unfortunately, however, as shown by several research studies,* Head Start children in some cases have not done as well in regular elementary school as children who haven't had a good preschool experience. Perhaps the regular school, which produces so much failure and so little success, is in morbid contrast to Operation Head Start, a program geared to giving each child a successful preschool period. Regular school, with its heavy failure orientation and its nonintellectual emphasis on memory and rote learning, hits these children harder than children without this *good* preschooling. Head Start children have been prepared for a school that does not exist, in contrast to the other children who accept school for what it is and do as well or better. For the Head Start children who do less well, the pro-

---

* Max Wolff and Annie Stein, *Study I: Six Months Later—A Comparison of Children Who Had Head Start, Summer 1965, with Their Classmates in Kindergarten* (A Case Study of Kindergartens in Four Public Elementary Schools, New York City), New York, Yeshiva University, August, 1966. Mary A. Krider and Mary Petsche, *An Evaluation of Head Start Preschool Enrichment Programs as They Affect the Intellectual Ability, the Social Adjustment, and the Achievement Level of Five-Year-Old Children Enrolled in Lincoln, Nebraska,* Lincoln, University of Nebraska, March, 1967.

gram is similar to preparing a soldier for combat by sending him on a vacation to the Riviera. I do not advocate doing away with preschool preparation for education; instead I advocate changing the schools so that they take advantage of, rather than nullify, the effects of excellent preschool programs.

What made the child so successful and so optimistic prior to entering school? He was successful because he used his brain to solve problems relevant to his life; he was optimistic because he had a lot of fun. He discovered that, although reality may be harsh, he could find ways to cope with it, ways that for the most part were successful. Most important, however, even when he failed, he was not labeled a failure; one way or another, harshly or lovingly, he was shown a better way. Even if his parents could not explain exactly why they wanted him to behave in certain ways, most of what he was asked to do was at least somewhat understandable. He was given many chances so that eventually he usually succeeded, but he was never asked to succeed according to rigid time standards such as school years or semesters. He learned to use his brain for its basic function: thinking. Certainly he cried, screamed, had tantrums, did foolish things, and was upset many times a day, but he did not make irrationality a way of life (even if it seemed so to his parents!). Outside his home he was less emotional and more reasonable because he soon learned where tantrums paid and where they didn't.

Children discover that in school they must use their brains mostly for committing facts to memory rather than expressing their interests or ideas or solving problems. Not so much in kindergarten, but beginning in the first grade and increasingly each year through high school, sometimes even through college and graduate school, *thinking is less valuable than memorizing for success.** The required change from thinking to memorizing

*The exceptions to this rule are in some of our scientific curricula, where thinking, at least the problem-solving kind, is still the rule, memorizing the exception.

comes as a shock to many children who have learned to think successfully. Many, perhaps a majority in wealthier neighborhoods, can survive this shock and learn to use their brains as the memory banks the schools demand because they have both pressure and reassurance from their families and from each other to do so. Without this pressure and reassurance, the children are more fragile, a condition common to the central city. When these fragile children, children with less parental and community support, are asked to memorize facts, they fail and they continue to fail.

Memorizing is bad enough. Worse is that most of what they are asked to memorize is irrelevant to their world; where it is relevant, the relevance is taught either poorly or not at all. Children are dismayed by the sudden and to them incomprehensible difference between the first five years of their lives, when they used their brains for fun and for solving their own problems, necessarily relevant to their lives, and their life later in school when, with increasing frequency from grade one through the end of graduate school, much of what is required is either totally or partially irrelevant to the world around them as they see it. Thus both excess memorization and increasing irrelevance cause them to withdraw into failure or to strike out in delinquent acts. "Smart" children soon learn that what is important in school is one thing and what is important in life is another, and they live this schizophrenic existence satisfactorily. Many, however, do not. I do not say that everything in school needs to be immediately and instantly related to the student and his world outside of school, but I do say that nothing should be taught in school that is not in some way relevant to the life of the student. *But this relevance must be taught.* Neither asking the child to think about irrelevant subjects nor asking him to memorize relevant facts will work; *we must educate him to think about relevant subjects.*

We cannot assume that children know why they are in school, that they understand the value of education and its application to them. From kindergarten through graduate school, we must teach students, or help them discover for themselves, the relationship of what they are learning to their lives. Our failure to do so is a major cause of failure in school. As our society becomes more complex, it is more difficult for children to understand this relevance. More and more they are asked to have faith, to learn material that makes no sense to them and often little sense to their teachers. For increasing numbers in our schools, whatever faith they may have had is running out and, with nothing to replace it, the only path is failure.

Not only are the thinking, creative, artistic, and fun uses of the student's brain drastically downgraded in school; equally tragic is that, in this mandatory group situation, little or no effort is directly devoted to teaching children social responsibility. Learning to help one another solve the common problems of living, learning that when we have educational difficulty we are not alone in the world, are ideas few people associate with school. For many, kindergarten is the last place where learning social responsibility plays any part in the regular program. Students are learning less social responsibility, not more, at a time when social responsibility seems to be at a low ebb. When students are not asked to think about the problems of their own world and about how they relate to the whole world, when they are rewarded for remembering what others deem necessary and important, they begin to believe either that right answers will solve all problems or, as they discover more difficult problems, that problems are generally insoluble through the use of formal education. In a world overwhelmed by social, economic, and political problems, *education seems bent either on denying to students the existence of these problems or implying that they are solved—a total break with the intense realities of our turbulent times.*

Our biological inheritance is our diverse thinking, creative, artistic, emotional brain. Our historical inheritance is an educational system that came into existence and survives on the assumption that the individual and his society succeed best when the skills and knowledge relevant to that society are taught in a formal situation according to a set of traditional values. Education seems to be moving in opposition to its historical purpose—learning to live in our world—as well as to our biological inheritance—the thinking brain. In the next two chapters I shall discuss memorization of facts and educational irrelevance to show how these antieducational practices are undermining our educational system, producing increasing numbers of failures, and handicapping most of our children.

CHAPTER FOUR

Thinking Versus Memory

In 1957 the Russian Sputnik showed America that others in the world besides ourselves were capable of intellectual and scientific achievement. As is customary (but ineffective), great effort was made to find who was at fault; why had we not been first into space? With our scientific achievements temporarily downgraded, the finger of blame was pointed at American schools, which were accused of failing to educate our children sufficiently in the hard facts of science and mathematics. This failure bore bitter fruit: the United States was second best in space. Educators with whom I have talked stress that 1957 started a bad era for the schools, especially but most unfortunately for the elementary schools. The political conclusion was that American children were being pampered with educational frills and social adjustment; they were not learning enough facts. Elementary educators were told to bear down, teach children more, make them work harder, and thus increase the information level of the elementary school student.* Intelligence and school achievement were more than ever correlated

* This is no figment of my imagination. Helen Heffernan, retired supervisor of elementary instruction for the State of California, did a comprehensive booklet on the subject that supports this contention in detail with quotes from educators, parents, and students. (See California State Department of Education *Bulletin*, Vol. xxxiii, No. 8, pp. 289-306.)

with facts, primarily remembered facts. School children were viewed as empty vessels—vessels to be filled to the brim with information. When the brim was reached, pressure was applied to stuff even more facts and information into the vessels.

This attitude, begun in earnest just after Sputnik, was intensified and supported by the emergence of the computer as our new intellectual god. The mass media in the past fifteen years have extolled the computer as the ultimate weapon in the war to solve our many problems. The analogy has been incorrectly drawn that the more our children's education resembles the programming of computers, the better will be the education. Perhaps the acme of this psychology was the intense interest in television quiz programs, programs that sowed the seeds of their own demise with the revelation that no human could be programmed to the extent that some of the performers were exhibiting each week. Although the quiz programs are gone, the public still does not know what was wrong with these caricatures of the educated man. We all have a little of the Quiz Kid in us, probably because the response to quiz questions is so easy to see and to measure. Thinking is intangible, hard to measure, hard to appraise quickly and simply.

Because of the difficulty in measuring thinking, there will never be an intellectual Olympics, although we do have Nobel Prizes. High school and college awards such as the National Honor Society and Phi Beta Kappa approximate more nearly the quiz games than high intellectual achievement, again (as will be discussed later) because the latter is so difficult to measure. The present system still says, "Learn as much as you can, remember it, give it back on examinations." If the memorization routine becomes too difficult, no one blames the student for using "ponies" and other educational aids. Perhaps no one expects that anyone can learn and remember all that is being asked of high-achieving schoolchildren today, so that even cheating, although reprehensible, is tolerated as long as it doesn't get out of hand and not too many are caught. The system breaks down tragically in cases such as the Air Force Academy's cheating scandals. Were the cadets at fault, or was the system? The question is not yet answered to anyone's satisfaction.

Today much of what we call education is merely knowledge gathering and remembering. Problem solving and thinking, never strong parts of our educational system, have been downgraded in all but a few scientific subjects. In many high schools, these subjects are considered so difficult that college-bound students often avoid them because they fear low grades. They stay with the safe memory subjects, reducing the potential scientific output of the educational system and thus, as so often happens, producing the opposite effect of what was intended. At all levels of education we have now an intense effort, perhaps reaching its peak in college and graduate school, to program people with predictable knowledge in the same way our computers are programmed.

Education emphasizes a lesser function of the human brain, memory, while relatively neglecting its major function, thinking. Although I wish to emphasize the need to increase all kinds of thinking in our schools rather than to analyze the various kinds of thinking, a brief discussion of thinking applicable to education is in order here. Most widely used in school is the thinking required to solve problems for which there are definite answers. Although thinking of this kind is fairly well taught in the schools in mathematics, science, and grammar, the answer itself or its form is too often more important than the logical steps to obtain it, thus downgrading the thought processes. Much less a part of most school programs is thinking that leads to ideas about problems for which there are no definite or right answers. We need thinking leading into inquiry about political, social, economic, and even academic problems for which there are at best a series of alternatives, none perfect but some, we hope, better than others. The war in Vietnam, draft procedures, civil rights, poverty, and lowering the legal age for voting are examples of problems that lead to much discussion but little agreement. Schools tend to shy away from thoughtful arguments, and in so doing eliminate an important use of thinking as a part of education.

Little emphasized but occasionally present in some secondary schools is artistic criticism; that is, thinking that leads to critical appraisal of literature, art, music, movies, or television. Critical thinking should be taught through discussions from elementary school on. As the arts permeate more deeply into our culture, students taught to appreciate them will be in a better position to enjoy the wealth of artistic offerings available in these days of increasing leisure time. True art appreciation is not learned by memorizing who did what and when he did it—the usual approach of the schools.

Closely related to artistic criticism is a fourth kind of thinking, which I call creative thinking. Students should have much more opportunity than most have now to create in art, music, drama, literature, and even movies and television (as the equipment necessary for the latter is more and more frequently owned by schools). Although some schools do stress these subjects now, they should be a definite and necessary part of school programs from elementary school through high school. Subjects requiring creativity are usually downgraded and considered impractical; they can, however, often lead most directly to the motivation, involvement, and relevance so important to the success of students.

Education does not emphasize thinking and is so memory-oriented because almost all schools and colleges are dominated by the *certainty principle*. According to the certainty principle, there is a right and a wrong answer to every question; the function of education is then to ensure that each student knows the right answers to a series of questions that educators have decided are important. While talking to elementary schoolteachers and asking them whether they allow free discussion in their classes, I have been told hotly by several teachers that they do encourage free discussion. They say, "We discuss everything until we arrive at the right answer." Although this attitude may not be typical, it certainly pinpoints the problem.

Children who come to school with the idea that many questions have more than one possible answer soon get over this idea. In elementary school, child after child is led to believe that school is concerned primarily with right answers and that teachers and books are the major reservoir of these right answers. The unusual child who questions the certainty principle by saying that there may not be just one right answer, or any right answer, to a given educational question gets short shrift in the average classroom. Unless this unusual child has an unusual teacher, he will soon learn that although his thinking may receive brief recognition, in the end, regardless of how thoughtful his discussion may be, the payoff is the right answer.

Not only does the certainty principle dominate the educational curriculum, it also dominates the rules of the school relating to the children's behavior. The children realize that they have no part in making decisions about their behavior or their participation in school. Taught formally from kindergarten about the value of our democratic way of life, children learn from experience that the major premise of a democratic society —that the people involved in any endeavor help determine its rules—does not apply to them. We wonder why there is so much confusion in our society over what democracy is. Could this confusion stem from the lack of experience in democracy in school?

Children should have a voice in determining both the curriculum and the rules of their school. Democracy is best learned by living it! Children who attend a school in which they are asked to take some responsibility for the curriculum and rules discover democracy; they also discover that in a democratic school, as in a democratic country, many problems have no clear-cut solutions. *Rather they learn* (and the ways in which this can be done in the schools will be described in later chapters) *that they have a responsibility for finding the best alternatives to a series of difficult problems, problems that they themselves help to pose. The process of stating the problem, finding reasonable alternatives, and implementing what seems to be the best alternative is education,* in contrast to the present process of blindly obeying (or breaking) rules and unthinkingly echoing back right (or wrong) answers to questions raised by others. As long as the certainty principle dominates our educational system, we will not teach our children to think. Memory is not education, answers are not knowledge. Certainty and memory are the enemies of thinking, the destroyers of creativity and originality.

In addition to the certainty principle, education, like much of our society, is dominated by the *measurement principle*. The measurement principle can be defined as "nothing is really worthwhile unless it can be measured and assigned a numerical value." Numerical values are necessary for comparison against another value or standard. The facts one student remembers as compared to others are the backbone of educational measurement.

During a recent visit to the Metropolitan Museum of Art in New York, I observed a dramatic example of the workings of the certainty and measurement principles. Wandering through the Museum, I saw a group of attractive young ladies studying picture after picture and then writing extensive notes in a school notebook. As I walked through the Museum looking at the paintings, I was puzzled by the girls' frenetic activity. In my ignorance, I could not imagine what a person could write down in such detail about a picture. As my curiosity grew, I decided to ask one of the recorders. She told me she was writing down not only the title of the picture, the artist, and general notes on the picture (this would have been understandable), but also detailed notes about the frame, which pictures it hung next to, and peculiarities of the picture itself. Her notes were intended to help her identify each picture when her art instructor at

Barnard College flashed a slide of it on a screen in class. She was preparing for an important test in "Art Appreciation." Evidently over the years the students had discovered that they could best identify the pictures by searching for certain clues in the picture itself, its frame, or its location relative to another picture. Their instructor was a follower of the certainty principle and the measurement principle. As I watched the girls busily searching for identification clues, I could not believe that their industrious note taking would produce an appreciation for art, artists, or museum. Although they were busy, they were not involved with the art. Using the certainty and measurement principles, their instructor is deadening his students' interest in art. At Barnard the students can choose whether or not to take this course in art cataloguing (assuming they know what the course is when they sign up, an assumption probably not valid for many). In our elementary, junior, and senior high schools, however, where most courses a student takes are required, there is no choice.

Let us examine how students react emotionally to the certainty principle and the measurement principle. Is what the Barnard students were doing at the art museum a happy task? Does it produce a sense of emotional satisfaction, a sense of accomplishment? Does it lead to motivation, through emotional satisfaction, to go further, to learn more about art? Or does it do exactly the opposite? Although it feels good to be right, if our correctness is based on memory alone, we have little lasting satisfaction. We gain more lasting satisfaction when being right is a product of thinking, judgment, or decision making. Without the external motivation provided by money, simple non-thinking gambling games such as bingo would not survive. Chess and contract bridge, on the other hand, are played in conditions of bitter hardship without any stakes and still provide great satisfaction. There is little satisfaction in being right unless thought or judgment go into the procedure or unless there is a great extrinsic payoff, usually money.

The girls at Barnard who get the answers right on the picture-cataloguing test will at best not feel bad. But it is unlikely that memorizing 175 pictures will make them feel good. Even if he is successful, the best that can happen to anyone who uses his brain exclusively to remember is not to feel bad. On the other hand, if he is unsuccessful in using his brain to memorize and has no opportunity to use it in any other way (such as thinking) , then he will feel bad indeed. Thus the picture-memorizing test, like most fact tests, is an educational dead end.

It is no wonder, therefore, that the memorization so prized in current education leads to boredom for those who are successful and to frustration and misery for those who are not. Memorizing facts cannot provide a deep-seated feeling of satisfaction—a feeling possible only when a student uses his brain to think and thus arrive at an answer or an alternative that solves a problem relevant to his life and to his society. Unless we can reduce the dominance that the certainty principle now holds over our educational system, we will perpetuate a system in which students gradually lose necessary internal motivation as they gain less and less satisfaction. We depend more and more upon external motivators—exhortations, grades, threats, punishments, and even suspensions—for those who fail to memorize at a level considered adequate by their schools, their parents, or themselves. The certainty principle, with its total inability to provide students with emotional satisfaction commensurate with their efforts, is an important cause of educational failure.

The failure is first apparent in the central city. Children there see little sense in working to get the right answers to even moderately difficult questions, although they do like to answer very simple questions. Teachers who teach right answers are frustrated because the children refuse to learn what they teach as soon as it gets above the most simple level. These teachers do not understand the motivating power of thinking. The children soon lose interest and, although their bodies may remain in

school, their minds leave. Outside the central city, where parental and community pressure to graduate with high grades
ranges from moderate to very high, many children expend the
effort necessary to get the right answers and to succeed in
school. The boredom and frustration caused by the certainty
principle, however, are reflected in home tension related to
school problems, tension leading to disturbed behavior seen in
the high incidence of delinquency in all parts of the community.

Surprisingly enough, failing preadolescent youngsters in the
central city express a liking for school; even though they fail,
they are in a well-ordered place where they are well-treated, a
welcome relief from home in many cases. In contrast, suburban
children in schools with every educational opportunity often
say that they hate school because it is dull and repetitious,
and it is not better than home. They have told me in class
meetings that they have much more fun in their well-ordered
homes playing with their many toys, with or without their
friends. Of those who don't say they hate school, and too many
do, few enjoy school. They look upon school as necessary economic preparation that ends with a diploma, a diploma directly
transferrable into money in the marketplace. Education for the
valuable and enjoyable activities of problem solving, thinking,
and creating is frustrated by the certainty and measurement
principles.

In terms of the psychological needs discussed in Chapter 2,
little of a success identity can be attained by using one's brain as
a memory bank. Merely retaining knowledge, without using it
to solve problems relevant to oneself and to society, precludes
extensive involvement with other people and with the world.
The certainty principle emphasizes isolation rather than cooperation and involvement. Each person has the right answer,
and the right answer has a value in and of itself, not as a means
to solve one's own problems or the problems of others. The

child, therefore, who successfully negotiates the educational system with a series of right answers in competition with other children seeking these right answers tends to become more isolated and to accept these right answers as the end result of his effort. Because these answers have little relevance to the world, he must seek most of his education outside of school. (Relevance, which is mentioned in relationship to thinking several times in this and previous chapters, is discussed in detail in the next chapter. Although I would like to keep these topics separate for clarity, they are inseparably entwined, and mention of one necessarily leads to mention of the other.)

Many children develop successful identities, but they do so in spite of, not because of, the educational process. Dependence upon memory leads to a shallow potential for identity. Education, which should be one of the basic building blocks of identity, often makes little positive contribution to the identity of those who succeed, but sadly enough, it makes a great contribution to a failure identity for those who fail. The sense of failure is much more immediate than the sense of success. This unfortunate situation has always puzzled me. Perhaps it depends upon the precarious nature of human relationships; so few of us have long-standing positive involvement with responsible people who value us. Although failure and loneliness are painful, they are easy; it does not take much effort to fail, it does take effort to succeed. As we fail, therefore, we tend to give up, to become more lonely, and to become immobile, prisoners of our failure. Like prisoners, we go nowhere. Thus, to a failure, success always looks so distant and hard to reach. The only way to reach it is to think, work, and relate to others, a far more difficult role for most of us than sitting in our cell bemoaning our fate. We see the increasing use of emotion in times of stress, the angry or withdrawn complaints of failures who do not know how to think effectively and who find no pat, school-type answers to their problems. In a society whose only hope is to solve rationally the complex problems that confront us, an edu-

cational system that avoids these problems, that does not prepare people to deal with problems effectively, must change.

People who find that their unthinking, emotional responses
are unsatisfactory learn to avoid new and stressful situations.
They thus restrict their lives, thereby thwarting the goals of
education. The goals of education are to give people the mental
tools to deal effectively with new situations, to place fewer
restrictions on their lives caused by fear of difficult problems,
and to enable people to deal with new situations and difficult
problems rationally rather than emotionally. None of these
goals can be attained by the present emphasis on the certainty
and measurement principles. The result of this emphasis has
been to cause some young people to seek illogical and angry
alternatives in problem situations that have no right answers.
Other young people are taking solace in drugs, in withdrawal
into unreality, rather than learning to deal intelligently with
what they complain are their problems and the problems of our
society. The use of drugs and alcohol is increasing among our
young people, especially among two major groups: (1) those
who are failing in our educational system, and (2) those who
see no relevance of the educational system to their lives or to
the problems of the world. Besides taking drugs, young people
who have not been encouraged to think in school, whose forma-
tive education years have been dominated by the certainty
principle, react with conflict, antagonism, and derision of social
standards and moral codes when *their certainty* that their elders
are wrong is pitted against the *certainty of their elders* that they
are right. Neither group seems able to use reason. Much social
and personal heartbreak is the bitter fruit of the conflict and
misunderstanding between the generations. The bland acceptance of conflict is too much a part of our society, a society that
will survive only through cooperation. But cooperation, a product of an intelligent appraisal of one's social situation, is poorly
taught in modern competitive education.

Although the few students involved in political action receive much publicity, a recent study done at Stanford University by Joseph Katz* reveals that most students have little interest in politics. Is our fact-memorizing, nonthinking educational system responsible for this apathy toward political responsibility? We need thoughtful liberals and logical conservatives, but we are afraid to include politics in the school curriculum. When citizens vote without thoughtful consideration, they elect politicians who promise the certainty of easy answers, quick solutions, and attractive images, all antithetic to democracy.

Worst of all, many young people avoid intellectual issues because they do not understand that these issues have no easy answers. When easy answers don't work or don't fit, they avoid the issue altogether. To counter the avoidance of intellectual challenge and responsibility, we must reduce the domination of certainty in education. As long as we look upon students as empty vessels to be filled with facts, as long as we train them to be computers to give us predictable answers to predictable questions, we are building into the most basic institution of democracy, the educational system, the seeds of its own destruction.

* *Growth and Constraint in College Students,* Stanford University Press, 1967.

CHAPTER FIVE

Relevance

In this chapter I shall discuss relevance and its relationship to school failure. Perhaps the best way to introduce the subject is to describe a class meeting about reading held with sixth-grade students at the 75th Street School, my home base in the central city of Los Angeles. On the edge of Watts, the 75th Street School is a 1900-student elementary school with all of the problems associated with a large school housed in an inadequate building. The students discussing reading had held many previous class discussions and were well versed in this technique, a technique to be described fully in Chapters 10, 11, and 12. Basically it is a method to get a whole class involved in thinking seriously about some important topic. The discussion was started with the question, "What is reading?" After a shaky beginning, because this was a new type of question to them, the students said that reading is what you do in school. You read your reading book silently or out loud, you read social studies books, science books, health books, and other school textbooks. Occasionally you go to the school library and you read *in class* some of the books that you take from the library. Although you sometimes take the library books home, you do so in relationship to school. The class also discussed the importance of reading and established that reading is vital because there would be much reading later in junior and senior high school, and the better you learned to read, the better you would do later.

I then posed the question, "Is reading important for anything besides school?" Further, I asked, "What would you do if the teacher gathered all the schoolbooks from every student in the class and said that from now on the only reading would be from material brought into the class by the children themselves?" I explained that the children would have to obtain written material outside of school and the school library and bring it to class to use as the school texts. The second question produced confusion. Many children thought I had proposed an impossible situation; without schoolbooks to read, school could not go on. More discussion followed of reading outside of school; some students did some outside reading, but not much. I was trying to get at whether or not they knew of the existence of important reading material away from school. Did they understand that the skill of reading could be used in their lives outside of school? After more discussion, they brought up the community library, but admitted that this was more in the nature of a right answer; for the most part, the library was also associated with school. Finally, I was able to separate them from school reading and its first cousin, library reading, by asking, "If you were given five dollars and told to buy a book, where would you buy it?" This question produced even more confusion, partly because no one in the class had ever bought a book (itself not unusual, as few sixth graders buy books) and partly because of their lack of knowledge about the whole process of buying books and of using money to buy a book to read. Most of them knew that bookstores existed, but only one or two had ever been in one. They had never thought that they might use a bookstore themselves later in their lives. Again, books were strictly associated with school.

The question about buying a book led to a discussion on reading materials in their homes. Where did these materials come from? Was there anything worth reading at home, any-

thing that seemed important to them? Part of the difficulty of
the discussion was that it was held at school; the children were
totally oriented to the too common idea that what was discussed
in school should have to do only with school. It was hard for
them, in school, to think about reading at home. Eventually, we
got into a discussion of the various reading materials in their
homes. Magazines, newspapers, cook books, Boy Scout manuals,
the Bible, and other material associated with home reading
were generally available. When I asked them what their
mothers and fathers read, they said, "The newspaper." Yet
when asked why their mothers and fathers read the newspaper,
they did not know. Most of the children had no interest in the
newspaper and didn't understand why their parents seemed to
read it with such interest. A few glanced occasionally at the
sports pages, about one-half at the comics, but for most of the
class the newspaper was something that existed for reasons unrelated to their lives.

I noticed that one boy sitting next to the teacher whispered
something to her and then raised his hand. When I called on
him, he said that he read comic books. I asked him if he enjoyed
the comic books and he said that he did, very much. Joining in
with some enthusiasm, the class revealed that almost everyone
read comic books, traded comic books, and even bought comic
books at the neighborhood grocery store. They were definitely
of interest to the class. I then asked them, since comic books
were so interesting, whether they brought them to school to
read. They said they did once in a while, but they had to be
careful; there seemed to be an unwritten school rule against
comic books. Some teachers (although not their own) took
away comic books when they found them. Because comic books
were scarce and the money to buy them was scarcer, the children were wary of bringing them to school where they might be
confiscated. I asked why in the world the school would want to
confiscate the comic books. The children replied that comic
books were bad; they were bad because they were nonschool

reading and had nothing to do with school. The children had adopted the moral equivalents *good* and *bad* for certain types of reading. Comic books were classed as immoral. Later, I found out that the boy who had first mentioned comic books had received whispered permission from his teacher to talk about them. He didn't want to mention them to me, in school and in front of the other teachers watching the group meeting, unless it was okay. The discussion ended shortly after I found this enthusiastic use of reading. These children had spent six years in school. On the one hand, what they read with most pleasure outside of school was not accepted by the school. On the other hand, what they read in school, mainly textbooks, was not related to their own world outside of school. Textbooks were only accepted and understood as they pertained to the limited world of the school, present and future.

To me, this dichotomy in the attitude of the children is a serious problem, clearly pinpointing one of the two aspects of relevance in the school. Supposedly, we go to school to learn skills to use in our lives outside of school, but the only association these sixth graders had outside of school with the most important skill they have learned, reading, was either negative (for comic books) or nonexistent (for everything else). In other words, their work in school was completely separated from their world outside of school. They believed either that reading was irrelevant to their world or, when it was relevant, it was wrong.

It is against this background of the relevance of school to life that we can better understand the reading problems of these ghetto children and other children as well. School education has become, for many, an end in itself. A major purpose of learning to read—enjoyment—is reached only through comic books by the children in the discussion group and, I presume, many others in the area. We refuse to see that for many, perhaps most, of the children in the central city, reading does not lead anywhere. And as most schoolbooks are dull, dry, and unemotional, reading stops in school at a level far below that needed for the enjoyment of books beyond comic books. Children need the stimulation of reading outside of school; but because they do not see the relationship between school reading and outside reading, and because schoolbooks are themselves relatively unstimulating, many children never learn to read well enough to enjoy anything beyond comic books. *They miss the whole point of learning to read!* Unless children can be taught with books in school that have the same appeal as the barred comic books, and unless some way is discovered to bring nonschool books of equal appeal into the children's homes, for many children reading will never be more than a school activity.

In addition to reading, the most important subject in elementary schools, we must attempt to relate every subject taught —arithmetic, social studies, science, health, and even spelling and handwriting—to something that the children do in their own lives outside of school. *When relevance is absent from the curriculum, children do not gain the motivation to learn.* As more complex studies come along in later years of school, subjects that only motivated students can master, the children stand still—and they fail. We cannot depend upon the natural curiosity of children to bridge the relevance gap because too often it fails to do so, especially among children whose backgrounds and interests are different from those of their teachers. It is much easier for a middle-class teacher to teach relevance to middle-class students than to ghetto students whose world she does not understand. She too often tries to fit her students into the mold of her own life rather than attempting to fit her teaching to their world. I am not saying that we must have teachers whose background is the same as the children's, but teachers must learn to teach more than what is important to them in their own lives.

Teachers are also handicapped by the almost universal use of textbooks and their belief that they should rely heavily upon them. Reading texts in primary grades are written for a narrow stratum of middle-class children who come from intact homes with no obvious problems, an unreal condition for half the middle-class children and for almost all the ghetto children. Although some new texts do show a few Negro faces, they are merely the counterparts of middle-class whites, a meaningless change. A better procedure would be to eliminate texts altogether and have each school district select books from the large variety of relevant, low-priced paperbacks now widely available. Paperbacks are cheap, they can be taken home, they are expendable, and they can be changed as needed to insure their relevance. The widespread use of paperbacks by the schools would provide an incentive for book publishers to provide more and better paperbacks at lower prices. When texts are necessary, they should clearly relate to the child and his world. To summarize the first part of relevance, then, schools usually *do not teach* a relevant curriculum; when they do, *they fail to teach the child how he can relate this learning to his life outside of school.*

The other side of the coin, the second part of relevance, can be explained with the example of a second class meeting held with fourth graders in a suburban school. The fathers of the children were successful professionals or managers. Advanced degrees were commonplace among the parents, and education was highly prized in most of their homes. In contrast to the students in the 75th Street School, who had had many class meetings, these fourth-grade students had never before participated in a discussion of this type. The discussion was held in front of a large group of teachers because it was a demonstration meeting and, as it was evening, many of the parents of the children were in the back of the audience. The children soon become involved in these meetings so that the audience has no significant effect.

I started the discussion with the question, "What do teachers want from children in school?" After some initial hesitation, the group responded that teachers want children to learn, to do

well, to get good grades, and to go on to college. The children
were repeating all the cliché answers that they had heard from
their parents and their teachers for so long. As I stated my
questions more clearly, however, asking what the teachers want
from children every day, they said that the teachers want answers. In response to, "Answers to what?" the children said
answers, both oral and written, to all kinds of questions that
teachers pose. Because I was pursuing a particular course, I
asked the children to discuss the kinds of answers teachers
wanted. Did the teachers want any particular kind of answer?
After a few hesitations and a few false starts, one of the children
answered, "Yes, what the teacher wants is right answers." When
I followed with, "Do you mean that the questions asked are
questions that can be answered by a right answer?" there was
general agreement that they were. I then asked them, "Can
teachers ask questions that do not have right and wrong answers
but that still can have important answers?" This question threw
the students completely off balance and they were unable to
recover for the rest of the discussion. Despite much talk, no
satisfactory response emerged. Because I was in a teaching situation and because we were in school, the students' orientation
was almost totally to right and wrong answers. One boy, however, said, "Do you mean questions we give our opinion on?"
When I asked him to continue, he said, "Well, do teachers ever
ask questions that call for the opinions of the students in the
class?" He thought for a while, and the others thought for a
while, and they decided that what they thought—their opinions,
their ideas, their judgments, and their observations—was rarely
asked for in class.

I was asking, and they understood this very well, not for
answers in terms of a first-grade "show and tell" session—what
we did at home or what we did on vacation—but for answers
that demanded an opinion of their own. Puzzled by my approach, because opinion questions had almost never been asked
of them at school, they were reluctant to explore the subject

further because they didn't think that their opinions were a proper topic for a school discussion. My question should have stimulated much more discussion than took place that evening. Their reluctance to talk about their interests, their ideas, their feelings, and their opinions was obvious as they shifted uneasily in their chairs, looked questioningly at each other, and generally showed signs of acute discomfort. Placed in a situation for which they were unprepared, they had almost nothing to say. They did not believe that their opinions—what they bring from their world to the school—are important in education. They could not see the connection between their own ideas and a discussion in school. Their own opinions, ideas, and judgments had not been sought for during the four years they had been in school, and they had no reason to think that they ever would be. The principal, sensing that the children were finally getting the point, went into their class the next day to continue the discussion. She said that she got an avalanche of response from the children as they began to understand that what she wanted was their honest opinion to an open-ended, non-right-answer question. Fast and furiously, as she tested one topic after another, they gave opinions on parents, teachers, homework, grades, and the world situation.

Here we can see the other side of the coin of relevance. School should be a place in which children can express their own ideas, based on their observations and experiences, and gain satisfaction from knowing that the school is interested in what they have to say. For at least five years these bright, eager, alert fourth graders hardly ever considered the possibility that school was a place for ideas and opinions generally, and especially for their own ideas and opinions. It was a place to learn the facts, to study the accepted and noncontroversial ideas of others. What they had to contribute, what they brought from their world, was not valued in school.

Thus we have both parts of relevance:

1. Too much taught in school is not relevant to the world of

the children. When it is relevant, the relevance is too often not taught, thus its value is missed when it does exist.

2. The children do not consider that what they learn in their world is relevant to the school.

Relevance, the blending of one's own world with the new world of school, was poorly established for the students in the second example and probably is poorly established for most students. The class even seemed a little annoyed with me because I suggested that their opinions might be important in school. They really thought it was wrong, almost in the same way that the students in the first example thought that reading the comic books was wrong. It's bad enough that the schools do not relate what is taught to the children's world and that the children do not relate what they learn in the world to school. But the wall of irrelevance is built even higher by the idea that what the children learn or do in their world is in some degree wrong as compared with what they learn or do in school.

In addition, the children in the second class were annoyed because I suggested that they stray from the safe, familiar, easy path of right answers to a much less familiar path of ideas and opinions. The motivating power of relevance had been effectively crushed. Secure in the world of school with its right answers and relatively easy school work, they did not want to relate their own lives to school because it might not be so easy. Of course, these bright children in a good suburban school were not nearly the problem that teachers encounter in the central-city schools. The children do have problems, however, although they are usually not serious enough to move many complacent suburban educators toward new ideas such as classroom meetings. The educators blame parents for children who do badly; parents accept the blame and, in some cases, take the children to psychiatrists, a fact I am aware of through long personal experience.

Most of these bright students learn the right answers easily, get good grades on the tests, and go quickly toward higher education. Unfortunately, these same bright students are now creating problems on most college campuses, demanding, among other things, that relevance be brought into their education. Recently, a poll was taken at San Fernando Valley State College, a large state college on the outskirts of Los Angeles. The main dissatisfaction the students had with the curriculum was that it was not relevant to their lives. Almost 60 percent of the students said that they could see no relationship between what they were doing in school and what they expected to be doing later on. They were bitter and complaining about this lack of relevance. If the anger on our college campuses seems out of proportion to what seem to be the problems on the campuses themselves, I suggest that the anger stems not merely from the irrelevance of the students' college education but also from their sudden realization that all of their educational experiences from the first grade on have been irrelevant. The anger is now bubbling up from the depths of these many years of educational frustration until it erupts in college. Students have a right to a relevant education. If we attempt to teach them too many subjects unrelated to their lives, they will invariably lose interest and begin to fail. In addition, we err seriously if we take for granted that students can see the relevance in certain material just because we can. *I suggest, therefore, that the teaching of relevance itself be part of education.*

The relevance of some material is obvious. To little children, learning to read and to do arithmetic is important. But they soon rebel against reading and doing arithmetic which they cannot relate in some way to their lives. If we can do nothing more, we should explain to children that what they are learning is a part of general knowledge that has been found to be valuable; that if they do not see its immediate importance, they must accept on faith its importance to their general education. We should also be honest and say that certain subjects are taught only because the students will be tested on these subjects by the state or for entrance into college. When subjects are in

the curriculum for reasons that we as teachers do not understand ourselves, we should tell the students so and explain that
we are required to teach these subjects anyway. If we have to
continue to teach irrelevant material, this explanation will
work to some extent. Honesty is a fairly good motivator if the
teacher has a good relationship with her class, if her class is
fairly intelligent and sensitive, and if she is able to introduce
some relevant material through the use of class meetings and
discussions. But honesty by itself won't work forever, or for a
curriculum overloaded with irrelevance. We must revamp the
curriculum or we will sooner or later lose the students. They
won't learn what makes no sense to them, and even if they
would, it would be a waste of time.

Working recently with a group of fifth graders, I asked them
what they were studying in mathematics. The purpose of my
questioning was to test for relevance and to find out whether or
not they were learning what the teacher was attempting to
teach. When the class said that they were learning Roman
numerals, I asked them what use there was in knowing Roman
numerals. After a long discussion, we could arrive at nothing
more than that Roman numerals were used to number chapters
in some books. Nevertheless, the class felt that they should learn
them because they were taught by their teacher, an excellent
teacher with whom they were closely involved. In my despera-
tion to try to get the class to think about the relevance of what
they were learning, I asked, "Do they use Roman numerals in
Rome?" Brightening considerably, the class decided that if
Roman numerals were used in Rome, it might be a good idea to
learn them; they would then be prepared if they ever went to
Rome. This seemingly good idea did not last long, however,
because one boy had been to Rome the previous summer. He
told the class that, all the time he had been there, he had never
seen a Roman numeral. The class was upset by this unexpected
information, although the teachers thought it very funny. This
example was not presented to put the teacher on the spot. The

lack of relevance in the mandated curriculum is not up to her; she is required to teach these subjects whether she wants to or not.

Although knowing Roman numerals may have some use, there is no reason to test and grade students on this kind of knowledge. In trying to use grades to force students to learn irrelevant material, we succeed only with those who are generally successful. It works just the opposite for the failures. We should attempt to break down the wide disparity between school material and the outside world. Children are stimulated by material on radio and television and occasionally by newspapers and magazines. The writers of this material would fail if it were totally irrelevant. The school should use the popular media and relate them to the school curriculum. Magazines, newspapers, and television programs should be used as an aid, not condemned or disregarded because they are considered antagonistic to education.

A serious failing in most school materials is that the emotion has been completely drained out of it. Emotion helps the child see the relevance of what he is studying. Most school materials have little or no respect for the children's culture, especially for its rich emotional content. Too much school material is unrealistic, unemotional, and dull. Unless school materials are changed, failures will increase because children seem unable to get started without the emotional bridge to relevance. Not only is emotion necessary in the school material, but emotion itself, so important in children's lives, should also be present in class. Laughter, shouting, loud unison responses, even crying, are a part of any good learning experience and should be heard from every class. A totally quiet, orderly, unemotional class is rarely learning; quiet and order have no place in education as all-encompassing virtues. To the degree that I have seen them practiced, they do more harm than good as they increase the gap between the school and the world.

Because it is so pertinent, I would like to end this chapter with the following quotation:*

The schools are no longer dealing with the student of 1900 whose sources of information were limited to the home, church, school, and neighborhood gang. Today's student comes equipped with a vast reservoir of facts and vicarious experiences gleaned from the new media. All the analogies comparing the mind to a blank page or an empty bucket died with Edison. The teacher is now in competition with a host of rival communicators, most of whom are smarter, richer, and considerably more efficient. Relevance and competence are educational tactics against which students have not devised a defense.

It is almost sacrilegious to find fault with Bel Kaufman's *Up the Down Staircase* because it is so human and so in sympathy with our own loves and hates. But the lady made me sad on page 198. "I don't think I got through to them, in spite of all my careful paper-plans. . . . The trouble is their utter lack of background. 'I never read a book in my life, and I ain't starting now,' a boy informed me."

Honest, Bel, they've got background; it's the one thing we're sure they do have. It may not look much like your background and my background and it isn't spangled with titles from the great books of the Western World. But it's there. We know for sure that it is well-stocked with plenty of TV material just waiting to be tapped with probing questions about phoniness and realness, winners and losers, style and schmaltz—all the new ways of talking about the old ideas of the true, the good, and the beautiful. If the school is in business to communicate with these students, it is up to the school to get plugged in to their background. Whatever the eventual goal may be, there is only one place to start and that is—where they are.

Teachers have seldom felt more alienated from the kids; yet it has seldom been easier to make contact with their world. We communicate with people by having something in common with them. One thing we can all have in common is the mass media. TV and film help to shape the dreams of today's students. Students often

* Father John Culkin, "I Was a Teenage Movie Teacher," *Saturday Review*, July 16, 1966, pp. 51 and 72. Copyright © Saturday Review, Inc., 1966.

have a kind of defenseless, direct, but interested approach to the media. They love to talk about TV programs and movies. They don't realize how much they're talking about themselves in the process. If the teacher doesn't watch these programs and if he never discusses them with the kids, he's missed the easiest way to wire-tap their private world. This is why all this élite versus popular culture business is so important. The snobs pride themselves on not watching television. Too bad. What happens when this culturally deprived teacher starts waxing lyrical about Elizabethan poetry? Not much. The kids have some polite teacher-talk which they dish out dutifully so that the teacher thinks something is going on in the class. If they like the teacher, they are very generous in keeping the truth from him. If they don't like him they still have enough fear for the sanction of the report card to go along with the game. They seldom say what they really think. Nobody wants to hear it, except, of course, the great teacher, who is by definition the relevant person, the one who understands, communicates, gets through.

CHAPTER SIX

Fact and Memory Education

Built into our memory-dominated and often irrelevant educational system are several specific practices that insure mediocre education. The general inadequacies of memorization and irrelevance were discussed in Chapters 4 and 5. This chapter describes specific educational practices that limit success and increase failure among students.

Probably the school practice that most produces failure in students is grading. If there is one sacred part of education, revered throughout almost the entire United States as utilitarian and necessary, it is A-B-C-D-F grading. Because grades are so time honored and traditional, anyone who raises a voice against them finds himself in the center of a hurricane; the defects of grades are so obvious, however, that many prominent people *have* spoken out against them. Some prominent colleges are changing the traditional five-level grading system to a pass-fail system.* In elementary school, grades set the stage for early failure in school. Students who leave elementary school a failure

---

* Some of these colleges (and this is not a comprehensive list) are: California Institute of Technology (freshman class) ; University of California at Santa Cruz (completely) ; other University of California campuses in some courses; Western Reserve University, School of Medicine (completely). Yale has adopted a five-year curriculum study during which time they will abandon grades except for honors, pass, or fail.

(which in many cases can be directly related to the grading system) will often never succeed again in school.

Grades were originally conceived as an objective measure (the measurement principle) of a child's progress. A child who brought home an A in reading could be certain, and his parents could be certain, that he was a good reader, at least as measured by his teacher. A child who brought home an F in reading could be certain, and his parents could be certain, that he read very little or not at all. Between A and F lie B, C, and D, grades by which a teacher tries to gauge the relative ability of a child to read as compared with an excellent reader or a nonreader. For most teachers this is difficult to do accurately. Students are often dismayed by a grade they believe is a poor estimate of their achievement. Grades are supposed to stimulate the child to work harder and to learn more, and to stimulate his parents to see that he does so. The child with the A works to keep it because any lower grade means he is shirking. The child with the F works to learn enough so that he no longer fails. If grades truly motivated students at both ends of the scale, there would be very little to criticize; but they do not now and will not in the foreseeable future.

Today, grades are the be-all and end-all of education. The only acceptable grades are good ones, and these good grades divide the school successes from the school failures. Grades are so important that they have become a substitute for education itself. Ask your own small child what is most important in school and he will tell you, "Grades." If you push him further, he'll tell you, "Getting into college." But you have to push him pretty far before he will tell you that he goes to school to learn, and he says that only because he knows it's the right answer.

Grades have become moral equivalents. A good grade is correlated with good behavior, a bad grade with bad behavior, a correlation that unfortunately is very high. Carrying the abstraction process further, we have made grades in themselves equivalents for good and bad without relation to behavior.

Grades, therefore, have become a substitute for learning, the symbolic replacement for knowledge. One's transcript is more important than one's education. The colleges of America which admit primarily on the basis of high grades are major culprits in an unpremeditated plot to destroy the students. Confronted with this accusation, the colleges argue that their best criterion for selecting students is grades; desiring successful students, they choose those who have the best grades. This reasoning, of course, is self-fulfilling prophecy because the colleges in many cases have become the pacesetters for fact-centered education. Naturally they want the best fact gatherers for their programs.

Grades are the currency of education. The highest grades are worth the most in terms of honors and entrance into better schools at every level. But because most grades are primarily measures of the student's ability to remember designated facts rather than to think, grades are often unable to indicate those who can do the most in the world. Richard Reynolds, writing in the *Los Angeles Sunday Times* in the winter of 1966, reports in an article entitled "The Obsession with 'Good Grades' Can Be a Harmful Classroom Disease":

A team of University of Utah professors made a survey of doctors in 1964 and came up with this result which it reported to the American Association of Medical Colleges:

"There is almost no relationship between the grades a student gets in medical school and his competence and success in medical practice." . . .

This astounded the leader of the research team, Dr. Philip B. Price. He called it a "shocking finding to a medical educator like myself who has spent his professional life selecting applicants for admission to medical school." And he added that it caused him to question the adequacy of grades not only in selecting those who should be admitted, but also in measuring a student's progress.

Just as amazed as Dr. Price was the leader of another research team in New York, Dr. Eli Ginzberg, whose group made a somewhat similar survey. That team took as subjects 342 graduate students in various fields who had won fellowships to Columbia University between 1944 and 1950. Ginzberg and his associates set out to learn how successful these 342 persons had become, fifteen years after they completed their fellowships. The discovery that shocked them was this:

Those who had graduated from college with honors, who had won scholastic medals, who had been elected to Phi Beta Kappa, were more likely to be in the lower professional performance levels than in the top levels!

Again, high grades were not a good indicator of high performance except in college.

It may be that in our current educational system, especially in higher education, a student has two choices: concentrate on grades and give up thinking; or concentrate on thinking and give up grades. Unfortunately, if he gives up grades altogether, he can never get into the schools where important subjects are taught; but if he concentrates all his efforts on grades, he can graduate with little understanding of how to utilize the knowledge that he supposedly has learned.

Another major flaw in the five-level system is that it is phony. That is, no one believes the formal definition of a satisfactory grade. The system says that C is a satisfactory, average, or passing grade; that the student who has obtained a C has demonstrated, if not excellence, at least proficiency in the subject. Yet no parents reading this book (and few children) honestly believe that C is a satisfactory, passing grade. When teachers and administrators defend the C, I have only to ask them, "Would you be satisfied if your child brought home nothing but C's from school? Would you consider that he was doing satisfactory, passing work?" I have yet to find a person say that he would be satisfied if his own child brought home nothing but C's. Certainly there are parents with an inadequate or disturbed child who would be more than satisfied if he brought home C's now, but they wouldn't be satisfied for long. They would only be satisfied with C's as opposed to previous D's and F's. Once the child started bringing home C's, the parents would clamor for more.

From talking to many children over the past several years about grades, I find that they believe that the line between passing and failing in our grading system lies just below B; that is, a child who gets mostly C's is essentially a failure in school because the only real passing grades are B and A. Thus the grading system sets the stage for failure, frustration, and lack of motivation. These results can be changed only by means of a different system that eliminates grades. If we failed those who did C or D work, the system would be exposed and soon abandoned, but we don't; we just place them in a position where, correctly sensing our attitude, they feel they are failures. After we get rid of our false system of grades, we must determine realistic levels of achievement, levels at which students consider themselves successful and our society agrees with them. How this can be achieved in a thinking, relevant education is discussed in Chapter 8.

Under our present system, students who have outstanding talent in athletics, music, or drama can achieve at least some success in school by means of these activities, even though they may obtain C or lower grades in academic subjects; all other C, D, and F students find school frustrating and unrewarding. Children with talent, however, have little opportunity to express it unless they get adequate grades. They are not even allowed in the door of certain activities, such as sports and drama, unless they show at least average grades. Because I believe that academic success starts with success somewhere in school, I believe that the rewards of extracurricular activities should be open to all. Although success in extracurricular activities does not insure academic success, it may make it possible.

Another sinister attribute of grades is that they are limiting and damning for life. In a world that sometimes judges people by their records rather than by themselves, a student with low grades has little chance to advance to higher education. While we preach that people should better themselves and that they should try and try again, we do not practice what we preach in regard to grades. Students with low grades rarely apply for the more attractive educational opportunities. They know that no matter how much their motivation has increased, their past will forever limit them. Although we know that people do change, that people mature at different rates, that temporary personal problems can cause failure not attributable to inability to learn or to think, the grade remains and cannot be wiped out. I have personally told students who had a poor start in college, and therefore feel that they have no future, to enter another college, start over, and never mention their earlier college experience. Some people may consider concealing the past (and my advice to do so) to be morally wrong, but to me it is a better alternative for a bright student than to limit himself to a mediocre future by telling the truth. People should have second chances, third chances, fourth and fifth chances, because there is no harm either to them or to society in giving them many chances. On the contrary, there is every benefit to them and to society in giving them an opportunity to rise above previous mistakes. As long as we label people failures at some time in their lives and then damn them for the rest of their lives for this failure through grades, we will perpetuate misery, frustration, and delinquency.

Grades are also bad because they encourage cheating. When grades become the currency of education, those who are greedy for riches cheat. Grades obtained by cheating (and it is common knowledge that many grades are obtained this way) are thus only measures of the person's ability to deceive. Quoting from another section of the Richard Reynolds article:

At least 55 percent of college students in this country cheat to obtain better grades.

That is a figure not arrived at lightly. It was established in 1965 after a two-year investigation at 99 colleges and universities by Wil-

liam J. Bowers, a Columbia University researcher whose project
was financed by the U.S. Office of Education.

Bowers interviewed some 6,000 students and 600 deans. He found
cheating at every one of the 99 schools and found it was three times
as prevalent as the deans believed and twice as prevalent as even
students believed.

Although grades purport to raise academic standards, there is
good evidence that just the opposite is true. When grades become the substitute for learning, and when they become more
important than what is learned, they tend to lower academic
standards. As long as grades remain as important as they are, few
students will study any course material that will not be covered
on a test and thus lead directly to a grade. Children learn early
in school to ask what is going to be on the test and, because tests
cannot be all-inclusive, they study only that material. For example, many teachers are aware of the hands that are raised
whenever they stray from the immediate subject, hands of
students asking whether the material is going to be on the test.
If it isn't, they may not listen because they don't want to clutter
their minds with anything not directly related to a grade. *The
counter argument, that if it weren't for grades they wouldn't
listen at all, is part and parcel of our use of grades to force
irrelevant knowledge on students.* Test or no, students listen
when the material is relevant. In many courses now the only
relevant material may be presented when a teacher unbends a
little and talks of what she believes is pertinent, even though
the material is not strictly part of the subject matter and will
never be asked about on a test. Where grades are all-important,
students tend to want to learn more and more about the less
and less that will be on the test, thus contracting education.

A dramatic example of the educationally restricting effect of
grades occurred in a class meeting with sixth-grade students. The
meeting was held in the evening before a large group of parents
in the Melrose School, a school in an upward-striving, middle-
class neighborhood. A frequent activity of the class of elemen-

tary school principals that I teach is regularly to visit the principals' schools both to demonstrate the class-meeting technique and to attempt to reduce parental resistance to eliminating grades. The statement with which I usually start the discussion is, "There are some people high in the school system who believe that school would be better and children would learn more if all grades were eliminated and only constructive comments were placed on papers and tests." Most classes, including this one, initially argue strongly against this suggestion. They say that grades are necessary to tell students how they are doing, that parents demand them, and that without grades students would stop working so that no one would learn anything. In the class of thirty-five students, almost everyone had something to say. During the first part of the discussion, every comment was a variation of the above defenses of grades.

I kept interjecting questions such as, "Couldn't you tell how you are doing without a grade?" Although some students said they could, they added that a grade makes it more certain. Most of them were steadfast in their belief that to depend upon each student to evaluate his own work was foolish as long as we had something as tangible as grades.

In previous discussions on the same subject at other schools, one or two students were intrigued almost from the beginning by the ideas behind my initial statement. Timidly at first, then with more energy as more students joined them, they would develop the idea that without grades students would be much more responsible for working on their own and that it would be good to learn for their own benefit, not just for a grade. At Melrose, however, only one student mentioned this point at all; when it was not picked up, it was clear that grades had a strong hold here.

As in previous discussions, I asked the further question, "What do you think the educators had in mind when they said that eliminating grades would lead to better schools?" I followed with, "Would you be willing to try it as an experiment?"

Previous classes could see the value of this idea and clamored to take part in the experiment, a complete about-face from their original position defending grades. At Melrose, however, these questions did not lead them to change their minds. They rigidly defended grades and their parents' wishes for grades. Over half the class said they would refuse to take part in the experiment if it were offered. When I asked how many would transfer to another school to avoid the experiment, about half said they would. Only two children, both of whom admitted they were at best average students, were anxious to try a new nongraded approach to school.

The climax came when I asked, "Since you believe that grades are so valuable and so important, would you like to have your teacher grade you tonight?" The response from the class was immediate and loud. Every hand went up, even the hands of two girls who had said nothing all evening. There were groans and moans, and as fast as I could call on students they protested. One boy who had been a vociferous defender of grades said that if the discussion had been graded, he would not have come. Child after child who had earlier spoken openly and thoughtfully said that if the discussion had been graded, he would not have spoken so freely. One child said, to the nodding agreement of the class, that it is impossible to have free discussion when it is graded. One girl said that, although she had spoken only briefly, if her comments were to be graded, she would not have spoken at all. She said, "I have found out that the safest thing in a discussion is never to say anything." The two girls who had not spoken had a kind of smug I-told-you-so expression on their faces when she made this statement. There was complete agreement that this had been a wonderful, happy, and open experience. There was also complete agreement that discussions of this type would never occur if they were graded.

After this dramatic demonstration of the effects of grades, there was little more to say. The point had been so well made that, in the short time remaining, the audience's comments centered around how we could get the school board's permission to do away with grades. Not one voice was raised in the defense of elementary school grades.

Although many people might agree that grades could be eliminated from elementary schools and perhaps even high schools, they would not agree to eliminating them from college or, more particularly, professional schools, because they believe grades insure student competence. As an example in answer to this argument, Western Reserve University Medical School has not used grades for at least twenty years because they found that students had so much anxiety over grades that they were unable to study successfully. When they eliminated grades completely and passed everyone except those who made no effort at all, they found that the students studied more and learned more. In most medical schools the threat of failure hangs heavy over students in the first and second years, resulting in much anxiety and reducing genuine inquiry and thought about medical problems. With this worry gone, the Western Reserve students were able to broaden their educational outlook, and professors were able to raise standards commensurately. In national testing, Western Reserve University medical students do very well; in addition, they remember their medical school experience as a pleasant time, in sharp contrast to the majority of doctors.

The final point about grades is that most teachers hate them. They believe they are harmful to education because they take time away from teaching; they believe they are inaccurate; and they believe they reduce the warm, human involvement possible and necessary between teacher and student. They continue to use them because they have to, but their hearts are not in it. Soon detecting the teacher's lack of commitment, students become good at manipulating teachers psychologically to obtain grades they have not earned.

The current grading system cannot be logically defended by teachers, administrators, or pupils. Most of its advocates are those who have long since graduated, who were successful in school and are successful now in later life, but who do not understand that their success is more in spite of grades than because of them. In Chapter 8, an alternative to the grading system is offered.

The second educational practice that helps produce mediocre education is objective testing. Completely consonant with the certainty and measurement principles, objective testing is the landmark of fact-centered education. Objective tests, except in rare instances, are passed by memorizing facts and regurgitating them correctly, a process that eliminates thinking by its total emphasis on the answer. A requirement to obtain correct answers gives little encouragement to students to think independently. School is often thought of as a place where there are right answers to relatively simple questions of fact. We should change this image by improving the questions to ask for answers involving thinking.

Although many teachers will agree with this argument for some subjects, they say that mathematics, for example, requires right-answer, objective tests. They are so oriented to right answers in mathematics that they can't see that mathematics can be taught as a thinking subject. Students can be tested adequately by problems such as, "How many math processes does a carpenter use when he builds a bookcase out of four eight-foot boards? Go through these processes, figure out a bookcase, use your own dimensions, and show how you would use math to help you if you had to do the job." Spelling is another subject cited by teachers who favor objective tests. Ability to spell lists of words, however, is often not translated into good spelling in written themes. Spelling should always be taught as a part of writing, as this is the only way that words, once learned, will stick with the student.

Objective tests, which by their nature deal only with the known, frustrate effort toward more thinking in school. All emphasis is on correct answers as opposed to reflecting upon important problems for which there are no right answers.

Thinking beyond elementary problem solving will not be stimulated in school as long as we rely on objective tests in which students are encouraged to think toward the known right answer instead of the unknown or the uncertain. Everything that is antieducational, even antihuman, is associated with never taking a chance, never broadening one's outlook, never looking into the unknown.

Objective tests discourage research, discourage thoughtful reading, discourage listening to anything but fact. Students learn to read their books by memorizing the words in italics, as if the author wrote all the other words just to use ink. I would hate to write a book, struggling over each thought as I have done on several occasions, and then know that the book was used as a basis for an objective test in which just the facts were selected for questions and the heart of the book—the ideas, the opinions, and the concern—was eliminated.

Many objective tests require little more of the student than memorizing the jargon of the particular subject, thus emphasizing words rather than the ideas behind them. Although every field of learning needs a few specialized words, many jargon words should be dispensed with. Teachers should encourage the unmasking and elimination of jargon rather than elevating it to the prominence it presently holds over much of higher education. Jargon is especially damaging and confusing in the social sciences, particularly in my field, psychology and psychiatry. Objective tests written in this jargon and calling for more of it in the answers perpetuate the practice. Essay tests in which the students' use of excess jargon is penalized would soon eliminate its use.

The third mediocre practice in wide use in the schools is the normal curve. The statisticians who discovered and the psychologists who applied the normal curve evidently thought they had the Holy Grail of measurement in their grasp. They found that, *given certain limited descriptive conditions,* much human activity would roughly follow the normal distribution.

Human effort could be measured statistically the same as tossing dice. Some of us could be boxcars or snake eyes, but most of us are sixes, sevens, and eights. If one had to devise a method of measurement to reduce motivation in education, the normal curve would be it. Teachers need make only a superficial evaluation of their students. They can doggedly point to the student's place on the normal curve and say that the student has no basis for complaint because his grade is statistically correct. Although the normal curve has been used to justify the accuracy and objectivity of the grading system, it actually underscores its inadequacy by making the A's and B's a minority of the grades and thus categorizing more people as failures than as successes. You can't beat the normal curve, especially when it is applied in situations where statistically it is inapplicable, a common occurrence in education. For example, a good professor teaches a course, stimulates his students to learn, gives a reasonable test (a test upon which all the students do fairly well) and then, following the normal curve, he gives low grades to some students who did well. This unfair treatment does not have to happen too often to destroy these students' desire to learn. The distribution may be highly abnormal (effective teaching should produce a skewed distribution), but utilizing the simple percentages of the normal curve, he gives the usual numbers of A's, B's, C's, and D's. His good teaching, his good student response, and his inadequate knowledge of statistics have produced a bad result. The students who did fairly well and still got a C or D must choose between two unsatisfactory alternatives: either study more than is commensurate with the course, or give up.

Finally, the normal curve produces negative cheating, a limited but significant practice in colleges where the competition for academic success produces intolerable pressure. Here, students give each other wrong answers in the hope that these wrong answers will lower the places of the others on the inflexible curve and thus raise the negative cheater to a higher spot. This sickening practice could not exist outside of the airtight vessel that is the normal curve. Fortunately, when A-B-C-D-F grades are eliminated, the normal curve will automatically fall by the wayside.

The fourth poor educational practice, closed-book examinations, is based on *the fallacy that knowledge remembered is better than knowledge looked up*. Most tests depend upon memory; reference materials are not allowed. I would hate to drive over a bridge, work in a building, or fly in an airplane designed by engineers who depended only upon memory. Engineers utilize handbooks and tables to look up important but hard-to-remember details. In my medical training, I have seen experienced surgeons call for a surgical book to be brought to the operating room when they were faced with an unfamiliar situation. I have seen other surgeons, products perhaps of too many closed-book tests, go ahead and continue to operate when they weren't sure what they were facing, at times to the extreme detriment of the patient. The world says look it up, don't rely on your memory. Schools say look it up, but rely on your memory any time it really counts, preparing the children for a world that doesn't exist. A legitimate rationale for examinations is to test how well we can use the tools of education. Closed-book examinations cannot make this test. Faced with a problem in life, we marshal all of the facts we can; we don't rely on our memories unless we have to. Tests are not supposed to prepare us for this rare occasion. Open-book tests teach children to use reference material quickly and efficiently, to give thought to necessary reference material, and to utilize facts to solve problems, develop concepts, and explore issues. Closed-book tests defeat all of these objectives.

Another important contribution to educational failure is the assignment of excessive, tedious, and often irrelevant homework. Whereas all of the bad educational practices described previously in this chapter have been used for many decades, the assignment of excessive homework is primarily a post–World War II phenomenon. Teachers in both city and suburbs complain bitterly to me that, in the minds of most parents, a good teacher is one who gives much homework; parents believe that learning is directly correlated with the amount of homework done by a student. The parents' demand for homework even extends to the primary grades, where children cannot understand its use or importance. Often in their attempts to work alone at home, young children make the same mistake over and over, thus learning and reinforcing wrong ideas that will be hard to change. Second and third graders are faced with parental disapproval when they don't work at home. Even when they do attempt their assignments, parents intervene, often taking over the assignment completely in an attempt to prove to an elementary school teacher how smart "their child" is. The parents' rationale for homework in elementary school, where they admit there is more than enough time to master the necessary skills, is that little children must get in the habit early of doing homework. As with many habits forcibly acquired too early, the later result is an aversion to important, necessary homework, homework that is accepted when the more mature child can see the sense in what he is asked to do.

The rationale for upper-grade homework can easily be defended. Students can't take their teachers home, but they can take home and read books, thus allowing the teacher time to cover additional material and to probe the importance of the subject matter by questions and class discussions. Home study also provides a chance for the student to break away from class routine and proceed at his own pace and, in some cases, use material of his own choosing. Good assignments that students understand and attempt to do conscientiously each night are valuable in education. In practice, however, homework assignments are often excessive and irrelevant. In addition, teachers do not correlate assignments, so that students may be overburdened one night and have nothing to do the next. Because teachers have little time to check homework conscientiously, rather than do good assignments students learn to hand in anything to get credit. Realizing that poor students rarely do homework, teachers gear the assignments to the A and B students who do the homework, thus widening the gap between the successes and failures in school. Shorter and more relevant assignments might attract the poorer students who could go at their own pace at home and might use home study to catch up instead of falling further and further behind as they do now. Although poor students as well as good students *should* do the homework, they don't; they give up. We must use homework in a way that reaches the poor students, or at least not use it to their detriment while we are figuring out how to reach them.

Almost all average or below-average students and many successful students tend to reject excessive and meaningless homework assignments. Their rejection of homework has become a major parental concern in these days of get-into-college pressure. In my experience, working with many intelligent adolescents, school and especially homework has become the single most serious cause of tension between parents and teenagers. When the child sees adults relaxing after a hard day's work, it is difficult for him to develop the motivation to do the long hours of homework assigned. Students who wish to go to college now must do it, but if they don't, we must do something more than say that they are lazy and irresponsible. Unless parents have an unusually good relationship with their child, they are forced to use threats, punishments, and bribes to attempt to get him going. Even these methods fail unless the assignments themselves make sense to the student. The result in many homes is increased bitterness and tension between parent and child. This occurs at a time when the child-parent relationship is already strained through the normal growing process. In my son's high school, an eleventh-grade history assignment was to memorize the names and the order of the presidents of the United States. When he questioned me about the meaning of this assignment, I could only laugh. He asked why I was laughing, and I told him if I gave that irresponsible assignment much thought, I would cry. When I tell this story to groups of teachers at meetings, I am overwhelmed with similar examples cited by disgusted teachers regarding their own or their colleagues' children. But if they themselves assign much homework, they excuse it by blaming parents who they say demand it.

Excessive homework penalizes the bright, creative student because, by doing it conscientiously, he has little time for other pursuits such as music, dancing, art, theater, science, and crafts. Students in many city schools must pursue these activities largely outside of school because the schools themselves usually have reduced programs in what are sometimes called "frills." The poor student doesn't do his homework, but because of his failure orientation, he usually has little interest in creative activities. His avoidance of homework is a total loss. The bright student interested in creative activities has little time to pursue them.

A separate problem concerning homework is that many students in the central city have less than ideal conditions at home in which to work. They are likely to be in a crowded home with TV and radio blasting and people running in and out. To expect students to overcome these obstacles two hundred nights a year is to expect too much. For these students we must either provide adequate public libraries or keep the schools open at night. A student who wants to study but who cannot find an adequate place to do so may give up. In a sense he is being penalized not for his school performance, in which he is equal to other students, but for his home situation, which is unequal to that of others and over which he has no control.

In discussions with large groups of teachers throughout the United States, I always receive spontaneous applause when I condemn excessive, irrelevant homework. Homework is just as big a millstone around the necks of teachers as it is around the necks of the students. Most teachers believe they could teach much more effectively if they felt free to reduce homework assignments substantially. Parents must stop badgering teachers into giving excessive homework assignments; instead, parents and administrators must encourage teachers to reduce assignments to what the teachers consider reasonable levels.

CHAPTER SEVEN

Preventing Failure—The Preliminary Steps

The Importance of Thinking

What is the educational potential if we could upgrade thinking, eliminate the emphasis on memorization, and substantially increase relevance? Let us examine how thinking, the most important use of our brains, has gradually been eased from the mainstream of education.

Although much thought is required to solve both the social and technical problems that face us, it seems likely that we will land a man on the moon before we solve the problems of racial discrimination. The kind of thinking that leads to the solution of social problems is more difficult but, unfortunately, less taught than the kind of thinking that leads to the solution of technical problems. Students who are taught social responsibility in school, who learn in a living situation to think of ways to help each other solve their problems both as individuals and as groups, are better able to help solve, or at least to cope with, the larger problems of society. We must get more students involved with each other in an educational system that seems important enough to them so that they will work to learn to think, to solve problems, and to become socially responsible.

No one can learn social responsibility, thinking, or problem solving when he is failing. The schools must provide all students who attend a reasonable chance for success. Because the problems of our uncertain world do not have straightforward answers, students must be taught to tolerate uncertainty and, in some cases, even to become positively motivated by the uncertainties of the world around us. We must teach children to think about the puzzling issues that confront us and confuse us and, in doing so, drastically reduce the emphasis on certainty and memory. School boards and administrators must acknowledge that ideas and issues are important and that children, from the day they start school, must think about them. Democracy is based on each man having an understanding of the issues of the day. He can develop that understanding as a child by thinking about various issues in school, provided the school issues are related to his life and his world as he sees it. Teaching the process of inquiry, we must show that questions are just as important as answers. Factual answers, the counterfeit currency of the educational system, are worthless unless they are integrated into ideas and thinking.

Not only must we teach children to question without fear and to inquire into topics they don't understand (and even that their teachers may not understand), we must also take the next important step of teaching children decision making and the ability to follow through on decisions. Time after time, patients come to my office failing in some aspect of their lives and troubled because they cannot make an important decision. Important decisions require strength, responsibility, and good judgment. Often, the patient seems to have some strength, some understanding of the facts, and even fair judgment, but he still cannot make the decision. I believe his inability to decide stems from a total lack of training for making and implementing decisions. Once a decision is made, a person needs the self-confidence to implement what he has decided to do. The required self-confidence is usually not developed unless the person has experienced success in school. Without confidence in themselves, failing children stall at making a decision to avoid the failure they believe will result no matter what course they take. School should provide an opportunity for thoughtful discussions on subjects that students have to decide about. Examples are whether to enter the service and delay college; whether to work while going to school; whether to stay at home or to leave for education, travel, or work; and even decisions on love, marriage, and sex. Unfortunately school, which should provide a forum for relevant discussions, plays little or no part in helping students answer these or any other social questions about which they will have to exercise good judgment or suffer the consequences.

Although the school should provide time for student discussion on all pertinent topics, the school itself must play an important role in helping students to choose a course of study suited to them. Despite the counseling department that most schools have for the express purpose of helping students decide what course of study to follow, the decision is often made hurriedly. The students believe that too little information is exchanged in the too-short counseling interviews. When students regret their choice, as often happens, counselors are too busy to help them make better choices. This poorly made decision in high school often sets the pattern for a series of inadequate educational and vocational decisions, almost all made in the same haphazard way.

Inability to plan and to make decisions derives in part from nonthinking education; planning and deciding are far more complex than answering factual test questions. Although a decision implies *an* answer, it does not imply *the* answer, it does not imply certainty, and it usually does not imply finality. Inherent in a decision is the process of formulation of the problem, development of various alternatives, and selection of what seems to be the best alternative without closing the door to possible reevaluation. When conditions change, and they do change, a decision that is in reality not irrevocable but that is treated as if it were, leads only to difficulty, sometimes to

disaster. A person or an organization who can reevaluate decisions and make new plans in the light of new evidence survives
and succeeds.

A decision must be based on an assessment of the applicable
evidence and facts. This is an intelligent use of facts; it is what a
computer does. A computer marshals the facts so that the person
using it can make accurate judgments leading to effective decisions. When our schools begin to train students to make and
implement decisions, facts will fall into place as an important
part, but only a part, of problem solving and decision making.

Parents and school boards firmly believe that they know what
is best for the children. These firm beliefs are usually expressed
by the schools sticking to safe, established facts and avoiding
issues, judgments, and decision making. A teacher in San Diego
spoke to me after a recent lecture to ask me how she could
introduce thinking when, for example, she was not allowed to
use *West Side Story* in teaching high school seniors; after one
parent complained, the school board threatened to fire her.
There comes a time when we must deal with ideas more real
than those in the story of Cinderella. If teachers with the
imagination of this teacher are not supported, education ceases,
not only in that school but in the whole district. Whether we
admit it or not, schools must deal with potentially thinking
pupils. When the schools offer little opportunity for students to
think about and discuss the relevant ideas of our time, they find
that many students either stop thinking, do their thinking outside of school, rebel, or withdraw, any or all of which cause
school failure.

In a system that deifies facts, it is difficult to challenge a
teacher who bases her teaching upon certainty. Fact-and-answer-
centered education usually settles down to a struggle between
teachers and pupils. The teachers have a clear upper hand in
the struggle because they know the answers to the questions
they ask, and the child cannot effectively challenge them concerning the questions they choose as important. The child who

complains about silly or irrelevant questions is overruled in any argument with the teacher. The system bribes the student by giving him an A for memorizing the facts. Because challenging the facts or raising issues not brought up by the teacher are good ways to lose an A, the student faces a dilemma if he wants to think. It is easier to take the bribe and keep his mouth shut, as the Melrose students explained in the class meeting described in Chapter 6. This kind of education is dull; it is no more interesting than baseball was when the Yankees always won the pennant. That fact-centered, nonthinking education is a prime cause of discipline problems and failure has not as yet penetrated the "safe" orientation of most school boards and some top administrators. Until they become concerned over the ineffectiveness of this traditional approach, nothing will change. Teachers, many of whom recognize the problem and would like to change their teaching approach, are powerless by themselves. On the other hand, if those who set our educational philosophy recognize the danger of the present course, the traditional power struggle between teacher and student can be ended. Gradually but willingly teachers will stop using facts, the best answers, and memory as weapons; instead they will work with students in a cooperative effort to wrestle with relevant issues.

Here again the subject of relevance necessarily enters the discussion. Teaching *irrelevant issues,* such as whether we should use land- or carrier-based aircraft in Vietnam, or *relevant facts,* such as that the war is costing $3 million an hour, is not enough. We need to teach *relevant issues,* such as why we are in Vietnam or why we should get out of Vietnam. In conjunction with the issues we can teach the relevant facts to support arguments on either side. When teaching encompasses relevant material and requires students to think about it, little or no external pressures, such as threat of failure, are needed. Students using their brains for thinking become involved and committed to schools that make sense to them. In this voluntary, internally motivated commitment, the student becomes involved with a teacher who is not an antagonist.

In Chapter 4 we stated that the best a student who memorizes facts and writes them down correctly on tests could feel was not bad. Thinking and involvement with teachers in a cooperative educational effort lead a student to feel good. This kind of education is psychologically rewarding because it allies with school the good feelings associated with problem solving. These good feelings lead to continued use of the problem-solving process. Students who feel good, who solve problems, who are involved with teachers in cooperative efforts, do not create disturbances in school. They are involved and happy rather than delinquent or withdrawn. Education has become interesting to them. Some people distrust interesting education and student-teacher cooperation and are apprehensive of students grappling with problems of our time; if we allow these people to prevail, however, education cannot help us solve the many problems that surround us. Schools that do not offer a relevant, thoughtful education produce many failures. Starting to fail early, the failures soon become separated from the successful students. Every effort must be made to prevent this separation. Unless both the successful and the presently unsuccessful students can become involved in good education, we will make no progress.

Heterogeneous Classes

Even with the opportunity of a good, thinking education, some students will do poorly. If we separate these students from those who do better, however, the lower groups will feel failure. Students, therefore, should be placed and kept in *heterogeneous classes*—that is, classes in which the students are grouped only by age. In high school and, to some extent, in junior high, some grouping by ability will occur as the better students select the more difficult courses. Because this grouping comes from the *choices* of the students, not from *assignment* by the school, it does not produce the hopeless feeling of failure that poor students acquire when they are thrust together by the school. Many school systems attempt to prevent excessive failure and increase ease of teaching by assigning children to classes according to achievement. These classes, usually called tracks or lanes and composed of students with similar ability, are established to prevent failure by setting lower standards for slower students. Thus everyone can pass. Unfortunately, even though they nominally pass, students in the lower tracks are treated as failures by the school and they consider themselves to be failures. One way or another, many teachers show their distaste for classes composed of apathetic or disturbed students. The days of these students in school are dismal and many drop out. Tracking not only does not work in the way it was intended, it works in the opposite way by increasing the number of the students who are failing.

Tracking, or homogeneous grouping by ability, is bad not only because of its effect upon students; it also has an insidious and destructive effect upon teachers. Where children are grouped by ability, teachers often do not appreciate and may even resent the effort of a low-track student who tries to improve. From the teacher's standpoint, it is almost as if a low-track, supposedly unmotivated student has no business changing his ways. This disturbing fact was among the findings of a research study of "self-fulfilling prophecy" in education done over the past several years at an elementary school called, for the purpose of reporting the study, Oak School, and located in a predominantly lower-class neighborhood in the South San Francisco area.*

The investigators selected at random about five students in each class. After giving all the students tests purportedly de-

* Robert Rosenthal and Lenore F. Jacobson, "Teacher Expectations for the Disadvantaged," *Scientific American,* April, 1968, pp. 19–23. Copyright © 1968 by Scientific American, Inc. All rights reserved.

signed to predict academic blooming, they casually told the teachers that, on the basis of these tests, the selected students were very likely to spurt rapidly ahead. The designated students actually had no more potential for moving ahead than did any other students, but the teachers did not know this. The results were remarkable. The designated students did in fact make great intellectual gains, both on an absolute basis and in comparison with the other (control) students. Because nothing else was changed, we must assume that teacher attitude in some way was able to fulfill this totally unsubstantiated prophecy. Not only did the designated students move ahead, but the improved teacher attitude, perhaps caused by the good news that there were several children with high academic potential in a usually uninspiring class, positively affected the nondesignated children, who also made significant intellectual gains. This study strongly points to the need to include in teacher training some insight into the marked effect teachers have upon students. Here the teacher's belief that some students had high potential was important.

This and other studies also show that teacher attitude can have the opposite effect. Teacher expectation of poor student performance that leads to actual poor performance *is* most prevalent where students are placed in tracks in the school. In the experimental Oak School there were three tracks at each grade level, a slow track, an average track, and a high track. The study is a damning indictment of how the track system affects teachers and how, in turn, their attitude serves to lock students into the lower tracks. The self-fulfilling and destructive effect of the tracking system is made crystal clear by the following quote from the study:

At the end of the academic year 1964–65 the teachers were asked to describe the classroom behavior of their pupils. The children from whom intellectual growth was expected were described as having a better chance of being successful in later life and as being happier, more curious and more interesting than the other children. There was also a tendency for the designated children to be seen as more appealing, better adjusted and more affectionate, and as less in need of social approval. In short, the children from whom intellectual growth was expected became more alive and autonomous intellectually, or at least were so perceived by their teachers. These findings were particularly striking among the children in the first grade.

An interesting contrast became apparent when teachers were asked to rate the undesignated children. Many of these children had also gained in I.Q. during the year. The more they gained, the less favorably they were rated.

From these results it seems evident that when children who are expected to gain intellectually do gain, they may be benefited in other ways. As "personalities" they go up in the estimate of their teachers. The opposite is true of children who gain intellectually when improvement is not expected of them. They are looked on as showing undesirable behavior. It would seem that they are hazards in unpredicted intellectual growth.

A closer examination revealed that the most unfavorable ratings were given to the children in low-ability classrooms who gained the most intellectually. When these "slow track" children were in the central group, where little intellectual gain was expected of them, they were rated more unfavorably by their teachers if they did show gain in I.Q. The more they gained, the more unfavorably they were rated. Even when the slow-track children were in the experimental group, where greater intellectual gains were expected of them, they were not rated as favorably with respect to their control-group peers as were the children of the high track and the medium track. Evidently it is likely to be difficult for a slow-track child, even if his I.Q. is rising, to be seen by his teacher as well adjusted and as a potentially successful student.

The authors do not try to answer the critical question of how teacher attitude is to be improved. For my part, the use of heterogeneous (nontracked) classes, as suggested in this chapter, as well as the other major suggestions of the book—the use of nonjudgmental class meetings and the abolition of standard grades—are all aimed as much toward reducing negative teacher attitudes as toward increasing positive student attitudes. When teachers employ these suggestions and succeed, their attitude must improve. *What we do produces change; what we do that is successful produces positive change.*

When we use heterogeneous classes we must be careful not to tell teachers which children have shown more ability in the past. Each child should have a chance for a fair trial with each teacher. Homogeneous classes eliminate this chance. In addition, even where heterogeneous classes are used, preknowledge of the child's past achievement evidently seriously restricts a teacher's ability to develop an open and nonjudgmental attitude.

Primarily from low-track classes, but also from heterogeneous classes with fact-memory education, come increasing numbers of children with such serious learning difficulties and behavior problems that a further group or special track has been designated, called "educationally handicapped." This phrase refers to a child so disruptive that he cannot be kept in a regular class at any track. Where funds permit, and sometimes by legislative mandate, these children are placed in special, small classes where much effort is spent to help them to succeed so that they can return to their regular classes. Not only does this often not occur, but the regular classes are helping to produce so many of these disturbed children that there is too often little of value for them to return to. Having been a consultant to a school system where such special classes are in operation, I am disillusioned with the procedure. Some successes occur where schools work hard to place these children back into regular classes as soon as they demonstrate they are the least bit ready. Generally, however, these classes become a wastebasket or dumping ground for the serious educational failures, a step before the larger dumping grounds of reform schools and mental hospitals. Special classes, where failure breeds failure and where the failures are isolated from the successful children who might help them, are a step in the wrong direction.

Even though the shortcomings of special classes are apparent, it is not easy to answer a teacher who points to children in her class so identified with failure that they have little control over their impulses and present an erratic, almost uncontrollable problem to her. She may conscientiously try to use the counseling methods suggested in Chapter 2, but even if she does get commitments from the child, he does not keep them and she becomes increasingly frustrated. It was to help reduce severe behavioral problems that I started as a consultant to several elementary schools in the central city of Los Angeles. Unless behavior problems were brought under control, there would be no education for the seriously disturbed children and poor education for those whom their behavior disturbed. It was immediately clear that these behavior problems were not going to be reduced by direct psychiatric intervention. We saw that we had to change and upgrade all our educational practices. One change was to abolish tracks and special classes.

To help get our schools under control, we placed the most disruptive children as evenly as we could around the school. We are implementing classroom meetings as fast as we can train teachers. In addition, we are teaching the teachers to talk to children and to counsel them according to the principles of Reality Therapy as explained in Chapter 2. We discontinued all corporal punishment and strongly advised teachers against using sarcasm or ridicule, both of which are as damaging as paddling. Without fear of punishment, children will enter into a dialogue with us so that counseling becomes possible. When they are completely disruptive, they will accept short suspensions—hours to a day to cool off—knowing that we keep the door open so that they can return by making a value judgment and a new commitment.

We know, however, that these psychological methods will not work alone. Unless children can gain academic success, they will continue to have serious problems. In the schools in the central city where I work and in most schools where children fail, the major academic failure recognizable to both the children and teachers is failure to read. Few problem children read well, many not at all. If children cannot gain some beginning success in reading, our psychological approaches will not work. Over and over in staff meetings we wrestled with the double problem of helping disturbed children and teaching reading more effectively. One conclusion that emerged was that many children, including almost all disturbed children, were not learning to read because they were far behind in their regular heterogeneous class. Sixth-grade teachers, for example, were attempting to teach reading at sixth-grade level to a class, spread over all grades in reading achievement, that averaged closer to third than sixth grade. Many children were totally discouraged and antagonistic because they were being asked to read above their ability. The teachers believed that if the poor readers were placed in a class where none of the children read better than they did, yet where most of the poor readers were not behavior problems, they could be taught to read. Remedial reading, the method usually attempted for those who cannot be taught to read in the regular class, is often unsuccessful. Children taken out for remedial work consider themselves failures in their regular class so that, although they may read for the remedial teacher, they do not read for their classroom teacher. The children cannot transfer their success in the remedial reading class to a place where they have learned they are failures, the regular class.

As we discussed disruptive children and poor readers in faculty meetings and as the teachers explained their teaching frustration caused by the wide range of reading levels in each class, we knew we had to change our procedures. We could not depend upon either the regular class or remedial-reading classes to teach these children to read. If we could somehow teach reading, the heterogeneous class could stand for every other subject. The key was to solve the reading problem; then our philosophy of *no failure,* the use of intense counseling of students by teachers, and improved discipline (not punishment) would together have a chance to help the seriously disturbed children improve enough to eliminate the special classes for them.

In an attempt to solve both our behavioral and our reading problems, we decided to place almost all children in heterogeneous classes except for one modification: the homogeneous reading classes. As a result of the experience we have since gained, I believe that *this special modification is not needed except where there are both many behavior problems and many reading failures.* Where these two conditions do not exist, homogeneous reading groups are neither necessary nor desirable. (Where there are only moderate numbers of reading failures, they should be taught through a remedial approach in which the remedial-reading teacher works in the regular class. This method is described in Chapter 15 on the Pershing School.) In many of our central-city schools, use of homogeneous reading groups in conjunction with heterogeneous classes is necessary and desirable. At the time this book is being written, our efforts centered around the grouping just described have reduced behavior problems and begun to get the children reading. We must recognize, however, that as well as this plan works, our continual effort should be to eliminate all separate grouping and use only heterogeneous classes. Because behavior problems and reading problems usually do not occur in significant numbers until the third grade, homogeneous reading groups are not needed in the first and second grades.

The heterogeneous class, a class of children of the same age, contains both the successes and the potential failures in the school. Each class has some bright students, some not-so-bright students, some hard-working students, some slackers, and some students who are obviously antagonistic toward school. Although these classes probably will be harder to teach when the system is first instituted, they have the advantages of eliminating early segregation for the various kinds of failures, of keeping communication open between potential failures and the successful students, and of eliminating from the minds of both the faculty and the students the idea that certain classes are the wastebasket or failure classes. When full use of the heterogeneous class is established, however, teaching will be easier because there will be fewer confirmed failures.

The meetings described in Chapters 10, 11, and 12 are held in the heterogeneous class. I have observed that, regardless of educational achievement, children get thoughtfully involved in these meetings; each child can succeed and thereby receives motivation for success. In any heterogeneous class, most children are well-behaved, setting a good example for disruptive children. Thus disruption can be handled as a classroom problem during the class meetings. In special classes where the disruptive children are grouped, there is often chaos or potential chaos that can be handled in either of two unsatisfactory ways. Chaos can be prevented by extremely rigid discipline that keeps children quiet but prevents learning, or it can be accepted using a more permissive approach in which some might learn but that very few teachers have the strength to stand.

In the previous pages I have explained the advantages of the heterogeneous class and the homogeneous reading group in terms of behavior problems. Let me now explain the academic reasons for this suggested grouping. I believe, and most educators agree, that in elementary school skills are far more important than knowledge. Although knowledge is of course a companion to the skill of reading, it is the skills themselves, especially the communication skills, reading, writing, and speaking, that are of prime importance. It is my contention that the first eight grades of school should be devoted to gaining proficiency in these skills. (I include grades seven and eight with the elementary school because no one knows what to do with these grades now. The best use for them is to sharpen skills prior to entering high school.) Reading is the most important skill for future academic success, but for success in life generally, speaking and writing are perhaps more important. Arithmetic is also an important skill for life generally, but higher mathematics, emphasized far beyond its real importance in most high schools and now in many elementary schools, is only important for higher education or technical jobs. Students who don't learn the essential skills—reading, speaking, writing, and arithmetic—fail in school and have much less chance to succeed in life.

Although teaching a heterogeneous class is initially difficult and often seems difficult whenever a new concept is introduced, the children remain motivated, there are fewer failures, and the faster learners can be used to help the slower, a procedure highly beneficial to both. Let us examine the individual subjects and see how they fit into the heterogeneous class. Reading is the most difficult skill to teach when the class contains children at many levels of achievement. If we separate the children into groups within their regular class, we emphasize the differences between the slow and fast readers, discouraging the slower students. The homogeneous reading groups, not based on in-class separation, are much less discouraging. Writing and its companions, spelling and grammar, are far more individual subjects. Working at their own pace, children are much less aware of their relative competence and do not become discouraged. A teacher can easily evaluate and encourage individual students who produce a wide variety of writing. Thus there is no need for homogeneous grouping. Because spelling and grammar are taught best as a part of writing, they automatically join writing in the heterogeneous class. Similarly, speaking can be taught best in a heterogeneous class.

Arithmetic also seems to present few problems in the heterogeneous class. Because it is systematic, it is less confusing than reading. Having learned about money through simple purchases, children have had a practical introduction to numbers and adding before school. Thus differences among the students are not as marked as they are in reading. Children who understand a math process are happy to work on their own while the teacher gives individual attention to the slower students. Arithmetic is self-reinforcing because the correct answers are available. Also, in arithmetic a child can skip a problem and go on to the next, but if a child skips too many words in his reader, he loses the whole sense of what he is doing. For these reasons, arithmetic is not difficult to teach in the heterogeneous class.

Science and social studies are more difficult to teach in heterogeneous groups because they depend heavily upon reading. To help the slow readers, the teacher can read aloud to the class and the good students can read to the slower children individually or in small groups. Class or small group discussions held after the material has been read can give the slower readers a chance to contribute good ideas to the class. Although teaching successfully in this way is not easy, it is essential if the slow students are to avoid the stigma of failure that they will feel if they are taken too often from the regular class.

The remaining subjects—art, music, physical education, and hygiene—are easily and best taught to a mixed group. The heterogeneous class, therefore, can stand except when there is within the class a great disparity in reading levels accompanied by behavior disturbances, a common occurrence in most central-city schools after first and second grades.

When the homogeneous reading program is used, the children have their reading level checked at the beginning of every school year and are then assigned to an appropriate group. Meeting for about one and one-half hours each day, the group works exclusively on improving reading. The children use a wide variety of reading materials, not only textbooks and school library books, but also magazines, newspapers, catalogues, and even comic books. In contrast to the heterogeneous class which needs to stay together for at least a semester, preferably a school year, to develop group feeling and responsibility through the use of group meetings discussed in Chapters 10 to 12, the homogeneous group is evaluated at least twice a semester so that students who are ready can be moved to a more advanced group.

Children beginning to read are taught in as small groups as possible. As they gain more skill and can work more on their own, the size of the homogeneous reading group is increased. For example, in a school where the average class is thirty pupils, the lower levels (preprimer, primer, first, second, and third grade) are smaller than average, say twenty students, while students in the fourth through sixth grades are doing individualized reading in larger groups of up to a hundred, perhaps working in the library. Children are assigned to their reading section not only on the basis of their reading level, but on the basis of their ages, so that older children are not assigned to classes with younger children in the lower levels. The mixture of children by ages occurs as bright young children are advanced to a higher level; it then has a positive motivation for all. In most schools where reading is a serious problem, fourth, fifth, and sixth graders reading at lower levels are in sufficient supply to allow the homogeneous groups to be kept fairly close in age.

Although children become involved with different reading teachers as they move ahead, their major identity is within the heterogeneous class. The homogeneous reading sections reduce the stigma that any child might feel who is reading books far beneath his age level because (1) he has a way to move up quickly, and (2) his major identity remains with the heterogeneous class because he spends only one to one and one-half hours a day outside it. Every teacher in the school and perhaps even the principal and auxiliary personnel teach reading to keep the sections as small as possible. The emphasis placed on learning to read well gives the program status in the eyes of the children. Placing all children in a situation where they are not competing against those much more advanced than they and allowing for frequent upward movement gives the program a positive direction. Reading is taught in a situation most advantageous to both pupil and teacher.

Children reaching the top level are all in one class, working independently. All students, some in small groups, some perhaps individually, have regularly scheduled times to discuss with the teacher what they are reading. Encouraged to volunteer as tutors for lower-level students, these upper-level students can increase the effectiveness of the program. There are no failures at any level; some students merely stay longer than others until they are ready to move up. Although it may be argued that those who stay longer consider themselves failures, at least they continue to compete against children who are no more advanced than they and they realize that they can work to move ahead. There is no system possible that can provide immediate success for every child under every circumstance. The suggested program eliminates failure and thus paves the way toward success in the most important subject, reading.

After the reading instruction in the homogeneous group is finished for the day, children return to the regular heterogeneous class to which they are assigned for the year. Within the heterogeneous class, the relevance of the subject matter and thinking are emphasized. Class meetings are held regularly. Those who do badly are tutored by the better students as a class project, receive help from upper classes as a school project, and are encouraged to attend short remedial sessions after school led by volunteer teachers on school time. After-school work is not mandatory but is available for students who need extra help to raise their levels of skill and achievement. The best use of these various helping alternatives can be suggested by the class during the class discussions that are a continuing function of the heterogeneous class. Students having difficulty in their work can ask the class for help; the class, during a class meeting, can try to guide them in directions that will help them to improve. In addition, any student and the problems he may have concerning the class can, with his and the teacher's permission, be suggested as a topic of discussion by someone else in the class. In the years that I have conducted such meetings, no student has ever objected to having his problems discussed. Because ways to help students are available, the class discussion periods need not be academic exercises; they can be planning sessions to help those in the class who are not doing well.

As I have previously discussed, the heterogeneous class is maintained completely except for the homogeneous reading sections. Although a child may be transferred to another heterogeneous class for a variety of reasons (for example, it may be thought that he will do better with a male teacher), he is not transferred for being behind in his work unless he is so far out of step that he feels total failure. In that case he can do better in a class where he has skills equal to some of the others. A child aware that he is not doing as well as some others, even in many skills (not in all skills), can be told that some go faster than others, a simple explanation most children accept. If the teacher emphasizes his successes (instead of his failures, as is too often done now), a child will accept the notion that learning takes place at different rates. This explanation breaks down completely when we use A-B-C-D-F grades because we cannot tell him he is doing satisfactory work if we give him a C, D, or F. The next chapter describes a system of grading that emphasizes success and reduces failure to a minimum by eliminating the standard A-B-C-D-F grades completely.

CHAPTER EIGHT

Preventing Failure—Further Steps

Abolishing A-B-C-D-F Grades

If we educate students to think, should we grade them? If we could be sure that each child would learn to think and solve problems to the best of his ability, grades would make no sense. Those who argue for grades maintain this rarely happens, that without grades students would have little incentive to learn. I believe that the kind of education offered (relevance and thinking) and the way it is offered (involvement) have much more to do with incentive than grades. When school offers little material that is relevant and requires little more than memorization, grades provide incentive for some students who get A's and B's; for those who do not get B or better, however, grades are a signal to give up. Those who get C or below consider themselves failures and stop working. They become part of the large group (in my estimate, over 50 percent in an average secondary school) who are learning very little.

Because grades emphasize failure much more than success and because failure is the basis of almost all school problems, I recommend a system of reporting a student's progress that totally eliminates failure. That is, *I suggest that no student ever at any time be labeled a failure or led to believe he is a failure through the use of the grading system.* As stated above, a student who believes he is a failure usually refuses to work in school. Because failure is never motivating, when we eliminate failure we cannot harm a child who is failing under the present grading system. Although he may not suddenly start learning when we stop labeling him a failure, at least we leave the door open for a change of heart later on when he may wish to start working and learning. If we label him a failure, often even once, there is less chance that he will ever start to learn. To keep a child working in school, we must let him know, beginning in kindergarten, that from the standpoint of grades or labels, *it is not possible to fail.* Whether or not any individual student wants to study, he is in a school where he sees many others who do work and enjoy learning. Kept in close contact with successful students in the heterogeneous class, he is stimulated to think during relevant class discussions. In this situation it is easier to succeed than to fail.

There is nothing radical about not labeling people as failures. In the armed forces, in athletics, in the arts, and in fact in most jobs, simple or complex, total failure is rarely of concern. Rather, we concern ourselves with levels of success; almost everyone succeeds to some degree in any job. Only in school are we so definitely labeled failure. For example, in a discussion of these ideas with a group of elementary school teachers, one teacher raised her hand and said, "Dr. Glasser, I *have* to give a certain number of failing grades each semester." I asked her what grade she taught, and she replied, "First grade." I then asked, "Does failing a first grader help him, help you, help his parents, help the school, or help the community? In other words, does it serve any beneficial purpose for anyone?" She said, "No." I asked, "Has anyone whose advice you might feel obliged to follow, such as a principal or a school board, told you that you must fail a certain percentage of first graders?" Again she said, "No," but added, "I'm still sure that's what I'm supposed to do."

It was obvious that continuing the discussion further would get nowhere because the teacher was convinced that she had to give failure grades. Apparently this conviction had been built into her over many years of her own personal schooling and teaching. A firm follower of the tradition of failure, she relied on the rationale that failure is traditional. It is just these traditions that have no rationale and that cannot be defended logically that set the stage for the many educational problems that confront us. The Rabbi in *Fiddler on the Roof* could not explain why men and women did not dance together except to invoke tradition (producing the marvelous sequence highlighted by the song, "It's Tradition"). Education partly explains its refusal to stop the labeling of countless children as failures by "it's tradition." This tradition discourages many little first graders struggling to make some sense out of a school situation they don't understand. Once a child receives the failure label and sees himself as a failure, he will rarely succeed in school. If, instead of quickly labeling a child a failure, we work with him patiently, he may begin to learn and, in a year or two, catch up. We have gained everything, lost nothing, by abandoning failure.

There are of course more arguments than tradition for continuing the present system—arguments about incentive, about fairness to better students, and about controlling the unruly. There are arguments that parents want the grade system and that colleges demand it. I maintain, nevertheless, that the price of failure associated with the present system outweighs even the most valid of these arguments.

I haven't met a child incapable of thinking and participating to some degree in school if we let him know we value what he can contribute. One of the best class meetings I have ever had in terms of thoughtful participation was with a group of mentally retarded children in a central-city school class in which their teacher helped them to experience success. I haven't met a small child who believes he is a total failure, but I have met some adolescents and adults who do. Having learned failure in school, they now give up all effort to think and to work effectively. They are defeated by failure. To correct this too-common bad situation, children, from the time they enter school, should be promised that they will not fail; to make this promise valid, they must not be labeled failures through failing grades. From the time they enter school they must think in terms of success, not failure. We cannot achieve this goal using the present grading system.

Failing no one does not imply that we lower standards or deemphasize learning necessary skills. We still must measure progress to understand where children need help and where they must do more work. We can do this through regular oral and written assignments that emphasize thinking. Children would be measured against a standard set by the teacher and then given more advanced work after they reach competence at the level of the standard. If one child takes a little longer than some others, it makes no difference. We do not have to fail a child or insist that a whole class work at the same pace all the time.

Even in heterogeneous classes, there may be a child or two whose level of achievement is so far out of step with the rest of his classmates that he can achieve no success at all. He should be moved to another class where he has some capability of achieving at a level of at least some of his new classmates. This change can occur at any time in the school year. (The end of the year is the worst time for it because it then smacks of failure retention.) If children are occasionally adjusted forward or backward during the year, and if they are also moved for other reasons such as personality clashes, there will be little stigma to moving.

Some teachers maintain that giving no low or failing grades to the slower students is unfair to the faster or the more intelligent students. There might be validity to this argument if it could be shown that the better students would feel harmed if the schools did not downgrade or fail their slower classmates. To my knowledge, such a contention has not been demonstrated, and I personally do not believe that good students look at education this way. The requirement for failure is almost exclusively an adult way of looking at school (and perhaps also at life), a way that we teach our children to their detriment. The good student works to learn and to gain the approval of his teacher and his parents. When he attains these goals, as he does by completing courses that have a reasonable standard set for passing, he is satisfied. If he is given a chance to pass and to avoid the C-D-F label of failure, the poor student, who now usually does not work at all, may become interested in learning more. Appreciating the value of a good education, the better student is willing to work hard, to try harder courses (in high school and college), and to learn because he enjoys it. I would like to suggest, therefore, two somewhat different systems of reporting a student's progress, neither of which employs traditional A-B-C-D-F grades. One system is to be used in the first six grades, the other in the next six.

During the first six grades, except for an occasional adjustment for a student who had nothing in common with his class, all students pass each year. Grade levels may or may not be emphasized. (The ungraded school, with which I have had no experience and so cannot discuss, is not essential to my argument.) Children are grouped only by age into heterogeneous classes and moved ahead each year for six years until they finish the sixth grade. Because there is no failure and no attempt to rate students against each other or against a rigid standard, report cards as we know them are not needed. To satisfy the parents' understandable interest in their children's progress, a written report is made emphasizing what the child is doing and where he needs to improve. The report is positively stated as, for example, in the following report from the University of California Elementary School:

AREAS OF EVALUATION

ACADEMIC GROWTH

Language Arts: Susan is able to write sentences and shows some understanding of the basic punctuation rules. Her ideas often show marvelous imagination and attention to detail. She needs to learn to organize these ideas and include details which support main ideas. She has a very good attitude toward writing and seems to enjoy working on creative stories.

Mathematics: Susan's skill in addition, subtraction, and multiplication is adequate. She is becoming more independent in regrouping in subtraction problems. She needs to review her multiplication facts in order to maintain these skills. Susan's attitude is inclined to be one of disinterest until she masters a new concept. She needs much teacher support and encouragement. She needs to set her own goals and become responsible for her own learning.

Reading: Susan seems to enjoy reading short stories from "readers" rather than library books. Her oral reading is fair. She seems to enjoy reading but needs to take responsibility for keeping records of what she reads and reporting on stories. Susan does need to develop better listening skills. She is often disinterested when a story is being read. When she does listen, she can recall main ideas and details.

Social Studies: Generally, Susan's behavior is still erratic. At times she is involved in class activities and at others, seems more preoccupied with her jewelry, clothes, etc. In class discussions, Susan sometimes makes relevant comments. Her speech is slurred and she needs to speak more clearly. She is working with a small group where projects are short term and pupils receive more teacher attention. This should help her to become more task oriented and involved in learning.

SOCIAL GROWTH

Susan seems to be an isolate. She doesn't seem to seek out friends or be sought out as a friend. She does participate in group games on the playground and seems to be taking a more active part than earlier in the year. She is usually cheerful and friendly but seems to prefer to be alone.

RECOMMENDATIONS

Susan needs to become more responsible for her learning. She needs much support and encouragement so that she will not become discouraged. She needs to review skills learned so that she continues to progress.

A report such as this one is sent home by the teacher at least twice during the school year. It need not be sent home at the same time for all students (an impossible burden on the teacher), but is spaced out, say, over the last six weeks of each semester. Thinking more deeply about their children so that they can write about them, teachers discover much more about them than they do using the present superficial grade ratings. The report is discussed individually with each student; parents are invited to join the conference, which are student, not parent, centered. As with the written reports, the conferences are spread over the last six weeks of each semester.

Recognition for Superior Work

On this narrative kindergarten to sixth-grade (K–6) report form, as on the seventh- to twelfth-grade form to be described shortly, there is recognition for students who do superior (S) work. This is reported in a separate paragraph at the end of the K–6 form as, for example:

Jane has, completely on her own initiative, written a series of interesting stories, read them to the class, and then worked individually using these stories to teach two children who were behind in reading to make significant progress. Jane, both from my view and the class's, deserves superior recognition for this achievement.

It is important, however, that the superior (S) grade not be confused with the A of our present system. To explain the differences, we need look again at the present system. A student with 96 may get an A and a student with 76 may get a C. Although both students pass, the A student remembers considerably more (at least for a short time) than the C student. Using S, a whole new avenue is opened equally to all students doing passing work. The choice of trying for an S is solely the student's responsibility. First deciding whether he wants to try, he then decides how to try. He must use judgment, make a decision, and think about implementing his decision. The extra work for an S is done concurrently with the regular class work. Most important also is the restriction that only one S is allowed per semester, thus eliminating the possibility of S becoming a substitute for A.

What does a student do to get an S? The principles of the S grade are exactly the same for elementary, junior high, or senior high school: for an S, a student does extra, superior school work on his own. If time allows, he may present his work to the class for both the enlightenment and the comments of the class. Final evaluation of the work, however, is made by the teacher. Presenting work to the class acts as a stimulus for more students to attempt work on their own. In addition, when a student attempts an S, he agrees to devote some time each week to help those students who are not doing well. As an example, a student doing satisfactory work in history may wish, at any grade level from primary through high school, to investigate some area of history that seems important and relevant to him and then to explain and defend his work. If his teacher judges the work superior, he receives an S in history. The student takes responsibility for his educational effort, sets his own standards, and does the extra work.

Using the superior system, extra effort is rewarded and education breaks out of the narrow confines of present practice. Superior work will come from students who at present rarely do anything more outstanding than memorize enough facts to get A's. In this system, S is not phony; it represents basic achievement plus increased initiative and responsibility. An S requires enough work so that students are satisfied to work for an S in one course each semester rather than the present meaningless competition for many A's. This system does much to rid education of the cut and dried sterility of learning details that have no value other than leading to an A or B. Teachers and students are continually alert for new ideas or new variations of old ideas. Good ideas come from elementary, junior high, and senior high school because *pass* and *superior* are real and motivating. The present grading system is a serious obstacle to improving education.

Grades in Secondary School

The grading system that has just been described applies to the first six grades. In junior and senior high school, where students no longer have one teacher all day but rather a different teacher for each course, several modifications are required. The narrative form of report filled out by the single heterogeneous classroom teacher is replaced by a form filled out by each teacher. Although it somewhat resembles the present report card, it differs considerably in emphasis and details. As in the first six grades, there is no failure, but all students pass every course attempted. Teachers set standards and *pass only those who achieve these standards*. If a teacher sets his standards too high, students avoid his courses or so many students fail to pass that parents complain. If a teacher sets standards too low, other teachers who have these students in more advanced courses of the same subject complain. For these reasons, somewhat similar standards are maintained throughout the school. Three possible report cards using the recommended system are shown:

History — S	History — P	History — P
English — P	English — P	English — P
Algebra — P	Algebra — P	Algebra —) *
Spanish — P	Spanish — P	Spanish —) *
Excellent Student	*Good Student*	*Poor Student*

* There is no record on the official transcript of these attempts in Algebra and Spanish.

A student who does not achieve the standards set by the teacher is eligible to take the course again. He is never marked "fail." A talk with his teacher can give the student an idea of whether or not to try again or of what he needs to do to pass. No record of his inability to pass a course is entered into his permanent transcript. School records are kept only of the courses passed and the courses passed with a superior grade. Each individual student, however, is asked to keep his report cards to present as he takes courses over again. These report cards are the only record of whether or not he has taken a course previously. If he does not pass after two tries, he must petition a faculty committee to allow him to take the course a third time. When a student leaves a school, he destroys his records. Although students who change schools may thus get a few extra tries, it is a small price to pay compared with transferring the damning no-pass record.

By using the reporting system outlined here, the destructive quality of our present grading system can be eliminated. Students who are slower, who may have had misfortunes in their home or family, who were ill, or who were not interested at any one particular time all have a chance to express increased or renewed motivation through taking the course again and doing well a second or even a third time. A school can find out about unsuccessful attempts at courses at other schools only if the student voluntarily shows his earlier report cards; the official record only shows what he passed, not how many times a course was attempted. As in the elementary school, a student is allowed to elect to try for only one superior a semester and, in electing to try, he must make himself available to help others who are having difficulty.

Using a system that does not contain failure, students are encouraged to try hard courses. Education is thus expanded. A student need not drop a course because he fears a low grade. Even if he does not pass, he can continue through the rest of the semester to assimilate a certain amount of skill and knowledge, perhaps enough to allow him to pass the second time if he tries the course again.

If the pass-superior system is put into effect, standards will have to be reexamined. Our present attempt to keep standards high is ineffective. Teachers present too much material and hold students responsible for learning more than they can assimilate. In courses such as chemistry, physics, advanced math, economics, or literature, a few able students keep up, but the rest fall behind and learn next to nothing. Recognizing that most of the students in these classes are incapable of performing at the required level, teachers give many C's and D's. In doing so, teachers achieve a perfect marriage between unrealistic standards and inadequate grades. Rather than take the honest approach—fail the students who know nothing (and almost all students who get C or less in any high school course know nothing in that course) —teachers temporize and give many of these students a C, getting both parties off the hook. The teachers rationalize that they taught a good course because few students failed. The C students rationalize that they did average work when in fact they learned next to nothing. The D students, who learned nothing, at least do not have to repeat the agony of sitting all semester in a class where they have no idea what is going on. The system is preserved, the only loss is education.

Using the pass-superior, no-failure system, teachers will not be able to maintain present unrealistic standards, which produce many students who know little about the complex courses they take. Many other students, knowing how unprepared they are, now will not take hard courses because they don't want a C on their transcript. We can continue to teach complex courses, but we must give students enough time to master them. This includes reducing the amount of material to be covered and giving the students more time to discuss the important ideas in class so that they understand the subject instead of picking at a great mound of subject matter. For example, my son's high school chemistry course was more difficult (more work at a more complex level) than the freshman college chemistry course I took at Case Institute of Technology in 1942. Students of today are neither that much more intelligent nor that much more motivated than we were in high school. The difficult course, coupled with the fear of low grades, frightens many students away from chemistry. Many of those who do take the course get low grades or need tutors to help them get a satisfactory B.

After he had survived chemistry with the aid of a tutor, I asked my son to take physics. He laughed at me. He was right because physics at his high school is even harder than chemistry; although he probably could have earned a C, it would have reduced his chances of getting into college. Also, he would not have learned enough physics with a C to make the effort worthwhile regardless of college. To repeat, then, we must cover less ground, *but we must cover the material we do present more slowly and in greater depth.* When students finish a course taught in this way, they will have confidence that they know what has been presented. When a teacher passes a student, it means that the student knows the course. The chemistry course, for example, could be reduced considerably in scope and complexity and have the unnecessary memorization eliminated, yet still give any student a good, fundamental foundation that would adequately prepare him for college. Using the pass-superior system, if a student took three semesters instead of two to get that foundation, he would not be failed or graded down. Although there could be a few special sections for those who wanted more advanced work, the regular sections would provide an adequate knowledge of elementary chemistry. Colleges would soon learn that a student with a pass from these high schools would have a good fundamental understanding of chemistry. It is not the college's prerogative to inquire if one student took a little longer than some others to learn the subject material. To summarize, let me quote a high school teacher who approached me recently after a talk in San Mateo. He said, "There are only two places in our world where time takes precedence over the job to be done: school and prison. Everywhere else the job to be done is more important than the time to do it."

One of the arguments against the pass-superior grading system is that colleges may find it difficult to screen students who have attended high schools where conventional grades are not used. I do not believe that this is a valid argument provided the other educational suggestions made in this book are followed. Colleges that want students who can think rather than memorize are more apt to get them from a school using the pass-superior grading system and the thinking education that goes with it. Students from either system will take the regular college-aptitude and other admission tests. To the extent that these tests require thinking, students who come from schools that follow the ideas of this book will do better. In addition, I suggest that high schools establish special classes for college-bound students to prepare them for these admission tests by learning to memorize the necessary material. Most colleges, unfortunately, demonstrate that they are interested in fact-memory students by using fact-memory admission tests. Some colleges use interviews; in these interviews, students who have participated in thoughtful discussions from kindergarten to the end of high school will have a decided advantage over students who come from conventional schools where discussions are rarely if ever held. Colleges often use an essay question as part of admission testing; again, students who have been exposed to essay rather than objective tests throughout their careers will do well. Colleges also want personal recommendations from teachers. Because there is much teacher-student involvement in schools following the suggestions in this book, admissions committees will learn that teacher recommendations from these schools stem from knowledge, not guesswork.

Although I have no intention of correlating the S of the recommended system with the A of the conventional system, certainly a few superiors on a student's record will indicate that he is capable of independent, responsible work. Colleges can also request that the high school office submit the work that led to *one superior* on the student's transcript. Examining this material, the college admissions officer can judge the quality of work done by the student that was judged superior. Although only one sample of superior work will be submitted, students can, in their interviews, describe other superior work. They will have much more to talk about than the student from the conventional school who has had little opportunity to do work of this quality. Taking all of these possibilities into account, I believe that high schools adopting the educational suggestions of this book will have no trouble getting their students into any college.

One major problem that I have not yet discussed is what to do with students who pass only a few courses in high school. Although I believe that the educational practices advocated herein will motivate many more students to succeed, there will still be some who are unable to pass as the academic course work becomes more difficult. We must establish a lateral direction; that is, courses at a simpler, noncollege preparatory level. These courses encompass vocational training and skill training in both the prevocational and vocational sense. Students can be counseled to follow these lateral directions so that they can succeed in the courses they attempt. Receiving diplomas specifying what they are trained for, the students will be better prepared for on-the-job training later. There is a level at which any student can succeed. Failure will not then be the roadblock it too often is now, denying many students vocational training by asking them to do more than they can academically and causing them to drop out of school. In most schools, a curriculum will have to be developed that will give every student a chance to pass some program of meaningful work—vocational, prevocational, or simple academic. Although we cannot maintain fully heterogeneous grouping in individual courses, we can do so in the home room, where students can participate in the class discussions described in following chapters.

Objective Tests

Adoption of the pass-superior system provides a more useful role for objective tests. Because we need facts to make judgments leading to the decisions of a problem-solving education, it is important that the whole class learn the necessary facts. Although an objective test is a good way to teach facts, any test that requires fact-only answers should be totally divorced from grading. Used as a self-evaluation tool in the initial phases of thinking and problem solving, an objective test makes good sense. When they don't have to worry about grades, students enjoy these exercises. Whatever the facts that each teacher requires her students to learn, they are kept in their correct context and not distorted upward as they are by the present grading system. If objective tests are used in any part of evaluating whether or not a student has attained the passing level, he should be given an opportunity to explain or expand his answers. Such a test should be short, with opportunity for defense and explanation both on paper and to the group. Although teachers may argue that time is not available for students to explain their answers to test questions, their argument is difficult to sustain. When failure is removed from education, time for teaching is greatly increased. It is the failing students who use up time and, for all practical purposes, the time they use is wasted.

As with objective tests, closed-book examinations should not be used to evaluate students. When it leads to learning facts to help make judgments, a nongraded, closed-book examination is helpful. It should be used only to help get the facts memorized, and then sparingly because only a few facts need memorizing. The important facts are remembered as students make judgments and decisions. In all discussions or tests leading to evaluation at the passing level, books, notes, and other information should always be available to students. Because reference material is available later in life, it should be used in school. The use of reference material expands education in contrast to the present constricting system of committing everything to memory. As the teacher should not tell a student what to bring to a test, neither should she tell him what *not* to bring.

Following the suggestions in this chapter will set the stage for changing the atmosphere in a school from failure to success. The wide gap between successful students and failing students will be reduced substantially. Teaching becomes easier and more meaningful because teachers are not caught in the continual controversy over grades.

Teacher Training

It will be easier to institute the educational changes suggested in this chapter if teachers experience such an education themselves. If they are subjected throughout their school and college years to fact-memory, graded education requiring little thinking and containing little relevance, they are willy-nilly trained to use the same methods with their students. Hopefully the day will come when teachers will experience a better education from kindergarten through graduate school than is available at present. But until that time, what can be done?

First, I suggest that an important part of the college curriculum in education be a subject called "basic education." Each student planning to become a teacher will be a member of an open-ended seminar on education from the time he decides to enter into the teacher-training program until he graduates. Conducted according to the suggestions of this chapter, the seminar will also provide for discussions as suggested in Chapter 10. With teaching the major topic, the students will discuss every aspect of how best to do it. As observers, students will attend classes, lectures, and seminars from elementary school to graduate school to study different teachers and their methods, evaluate what they have observed, and bring these observations and evaluations to the seminar. College professors, public school teachers and, most of all, students from all levels of education will be invited periodically to participate in the seminar in a mutual effort to discover the best approaches to teaching at all levels and in various subjects. Such a series of discussions will lead, not to absolute solutions, but to many good teaching alternatives that can be applied by each student according to his own personality. This same kind of seminar should be conducted within each school system; for at least two years each new teacher will be a member of a group led by paid master teachers of the district. The performance of the new teacher in the seminar group should not be part of his evaluation for tenure. The whole emphasis of the seminar should be on the effectiveness of each member as a teacher.

The second suggestion on improving teacher training is for students to take few formal college courses in education other than the suggested basic-education seminar and that they spend the time instead in additional practice teaching. In this way they could spend a full year rather than just one semester in practice teaching. Discussion of the practice teaching should be part of the basic-education seminar so that everyone could learn which techniques the students use are effective and which are not. Unfortunately, most teachers enter the profession with limited experience under the supervision of seasoned teachers. New teachers should have much more experience under supervision, both during their training and during their probationary period. Grading and evaluating should be eliminated so that the new teachers can experiment with various methods without fear of criticism. The fear of graded criticism, gained through the period of student teaching, is difficult to remove once the teacher begins his permanent career. Teachers often then conduct their classes so that their students are hesitant to speak for fear of being graded on whatever they may say.

Although the suggestions made here are limited, they are intended to pinpoint the need to improve teacher training. If teacher training is not improved, it will be difficult to carry through the many changes needed in the schools.

CHAPTER NINE

Implementing New Programs

In earlier chapters many suggestions have been made for changing school procedures to reduce school failure. In the following three chapters, class meetings, previously mentioned as a way to get students involved in relevant discussions, are described. When I discuss these ideas with school teachers and administrators, I am often told, "These suggestions are great, but we will never get them going here." The attitude is that it is next to impossible to change the *status quo*.

Because I am trying to effect change, I wish to examine why new ideas move slowly into the schools. Dr. H. Thomas James, Dean of the Stanford School of Education, recently commented on the situation in which supervisors, resource specialists, curriculum consultants, and other experts are busy proposing changes, "but when teachers get out of their meetings and close the door to their classrooms, things go on pretty much as they have for decades in most schools." My own limited experience fully confirms Dean James's observation.

On the basis of my experience working in the schools, I would like to make some suggestions that I hope can lead the schools to do more than pay lip service to the need to change their traditional methods. One major obstacle to starting new programs and using new approaches is that most educational thinking is taking place in schools of education affiliated for training and research with middle- and upper-class school systems. Because these systems are generally doing a fairly satisfactory job of traditional fact-memory education, there is little incentive for change. Where education is a failure, as in the central city, little that is new is tried because the innovators don't work in these schools long enough to effect change and because the teachers resist innovation, which they fear will make their job harder. Teachers complain that they can barely survive the school day without worrying about suggestions from outsiders who, they believe, don't understand their problems anyway. Thus in suburbia, where the children memorize the facts and don't complain too much about the lack of relevance, teachers don't wish to rock the boat and try new approaches. Where education is failing, teachers are too overworked and discouraged to try anything new. If education in suburbia were as dismal as it is in the central city, parents would be breaking down the walls with their complaints. If city education were as successful as suburban education appears to be, we would be less concerned than we are. The central-city parents do not complain for two reasons: they cannot compare their children's failure with a successful school experience of their own, most of them having themselves failed in school; and they have no political organization or political power.

The dismal state of education in the central city, recognized more clearly by educators than by students and parents, has given me the chance to work in the schools; similarly, the serious problems of rehabilitating adolescent girls gave me the opportunity to work at the Ventura School. Opportunities to develop and implement new ideas are not often available. Thus the only bright spot in the failure of central-city education is that the need for change is apparent to thoughtful teachers and administrators; parents and students are also beginning to see this same need. Educational advances will rarely come from complacent suburbia. They will come from the city or probably not at all.

What are the problems faced by anyone trying to get teachers to use new ideas and new programs? Although they are confronted with serious failure in the central city and considerable failure in the suburbs, teachers nevertheless feel threatened by anyone who suggests basic changes in methods of teaching or in the school curriculum. It is hard to describe the atmosphere that I find initially in most schools. There seems to be resignation to the *status quo* and, despite some dissatisfaction with present practices, antagonism toward anyone who advocates change. The reluctance to change extends not only to the practices with which the faculty agree, but even to those with which they disagree.

Administrators express the same attitude to a lesser degree. They blame teachers and parents for their inability to change the program. Similarly, parents blame administrators and teachers for not instituting changes. Thus we have a complete circle in which teachers blame parents and administrators, administrators blame teachers and parents, and parents blame teachers and administrators.

Underlying the resistance to change is a general attitude probably induced by the atmosphere of grades and failure that dominates both the students and the teachers. This attitude, acting as a barrier to change, was mentioned in Chapter 8 as an attitude that leads to poor teaching. Because everyone in the school is so preoccupied with failure and grades, teachers fear that anything they do will be discovered, graded, and then criticized (failed) as an unwise step by their principal or by a dissatisfied parent who complains to the principal. Teachers avoid making changes so that no one will consider them failures if the new program is not perfect.

Fear of change is less among administrators than among teachers, and it is less among good teachers supported by good

administrators. Even when there is a definite desire by both
teachers and administrators to change, the main obstacle to
implementing new ideas is the teachers' lack of confidence in
administrative support. Administrators must make the scope
and content of proposed changes clear and give them strong and
continued support. Brief memoranda and short discussions will
not suffice.

Although it is desirable that change come from the needs of
the faculty, we cannot depend upon any one group to recognize
all that may be needed. The homogeneous-group reading program discussed in the previous chapter is an example of a
change suggested by the teachers. The program was developed
as a result of a series of faculty discussions about the difficulty of
teaching reading. Dissatisfied with the reading program as it
existed, the teachers quickly implemented the new program.
On the other hand, the class meetings discussed in the next
three chapters have been difficult to get started because teachers
cannot see the value of this new program before they try it.
Having had little personal experience with thoughtful discussions, they feel inadequately prepared to lead their classes. Fear-
ing failure, they tend to resist starting class discussions. Surprisingly, the major resistance has been toward the moving of the
class into the circle necessary for a good discussion. Teacher
after teacher who complains of failure in her attempts to lead a
class meeting has admitted that she has not formed her class into
the discussion circle. She attempts to use some other seating
arrangement or she attempts to hold discussions in the regular
seating arrangement of rows, an almost insurmountable obstacle
to a good discussion. Teachers resist my suggestion despite my
repeated statements that I have never held a successful meeting
when the class was not in a circle. Several principals have told
me flatly that some teachers will not move their classes into a
circle. The refusal to perform such a seemingly mechanical
procedure, which takes no more than 90 seconds of class time
the first time it is done and less time thereafter, illustrates the

resistance to change when teachers are unsure of a new teaching procedure. Attempting to overcome the teachers' resistance to forming the class into the circle, I now demonstrate not only how to conduct the meeting but also how to get the class into the circle. Gratifying to me is the success and satisfaction experienced by teachers who follow this and the other suggestions for conducting the class meetings.

Change, therefore, is best initiated as a result of teachers meeting together to solve problems. The teachers themselves must get involved with the need for changes and the desirability of new programs. They must be taught patiently and consistently how to implement any suggested changes. In addition, to help them implement their own ideas they must be organized into discussion groups. For any new program to be successful, the teachers must themselves believe that it is meaningful. Lack of relevance to teachers causes the failure of many new approaches. The "new math" is an excellent example of a new approach that teachers don't understand and often teach poorly because they doubt its value.

A brief clarification is needed here about the responsibility for initiating change. Teachers as a group should have the opportunity to bring their proposals to faculty meetings for discussion and to initiate changes. On their own, they should be allowed to make changes as major as abandoning reading textbooks and developing a reading curriculum using home, library, and school reference resources. The results of such new methods should be presented to the faculty. Teachers, however, cannot be responsible for all changes and need not agree with every change proposed by the administration. Class meetings, for example, would never occur if their introduction were left to teachers alone. Instituting class meetings is an administrator's proposal to which teachers must concur and then be helped to implement. In such a change, the teachers' concurrence is necessary; no administrator can force his faculty to conduct class meetings against their will.

Some major changes, such as the abandonment of graded report cards, can be initiated and carried through satisfactorily by administrative order. I have recently been involved in eliminating or modifying report cards in several schools. In one school, when the order that there would be no more report cards came from the principal, the teachers worked to develop a new method of reporting to parents. Conferences with parents were agreed upon. On the other hand, when in another school we asked the faculty to recommend a better method than the present A-B-C-D-F report cards, there was so much wrangling that it was impossible to implement any new grading method. Unlike starting class meetings, grades can be eliminated administratively. Although faculty cooperation is helpful in making all changes, it is vital only when something new is added. Removing traditional practices such as grades requires only a strong administration and the opportunity for teachers to work toward an alternative.

In most schools it is difficult for changes to get started because one of the requisites for change—that teachers have time to meet as a group—is not met. Teachers need time to discuss, develop, and accept new approaches, to see demonstrations, and to receive repeated instruction. Instead of a working, cohesive, problem-solving faculty group, most faculties consist of teachers working alone in their classes, each doing the best she can with little knowledge or understanding of what the other teachers in the school are doing. Although each teacher works toward the vague but rarely questioned goal of bringing her students to grade level, few teachers consider how their students were taught before they came to each one or how they will be taught after they move on to the next grade. All schools need regularly scheduled faculty meetings to develop an educational philosophy for the school. Once a working philosophy is agreed upon, it should be implemented by using new approaches and new techniques where old ones have not done the job. The schools differ, not only from most businesses, but from all other

agencies that work to improve human behavior in that little or
no working time is devoted to staff meetings. Unless the teachers can meet together and as committees work with the principal and with the grade-level chairmen to develop programs to
solve educational problems, nothing new will happen. I hesitate
to write the previous sentence because so many readers have had
bad experience with committees that waste time and accomplish
little. Unless school committees are given a mandate to implement their recommendations, they too will be meaningless.

At present the contact among teachers in the average school is
so limited that few have ever seen another teacher teach. In
addition, almost no teacher is comfortable when the principal is
in her class. There is little group feeling; each teacher is concerned almost exclusively with her own problems. The more we
are able to break this wall of isolation so that teachers can see
each other teach and can learn from each other, the better education will be. An excellent example of a school in which
teachers help each other is the Pershing School, discussed in
Chapter 15.

One of the most disturbing ways to conduct a meeting of
educators is to ask them to discuss their educational philosophy
and, as the discussion proceeds, write the points brought up on
the blackboard. I used this procedure recently with a large
group of elementary school administrators who, after some
trouble getting started, developed an excellent list of educational goals. Among them were most of the ideas advanced in
previous chapters of this book including concern for thinking,
for the individual child, for relevant education, and for success
for all students. When the discussion was an hour old, one
principal who had not previously spoken raised his hand and
said that the group had certainly produced a wonderful list, but
that the items listed were not happening in his school. After
some nervous laughter, there was an uncomfortable but honest
agreement that education in their schools consisted more of fact
memorizing, lack of involvement, and failure than it did of the

philosophy written on the board. It was then easy to get agreement that we must discover for ourselves or from others the flaws in our programs and then close the gap between what we believe is good education and what we practice. This gap is not closed, not only because principals and teachers do not have the time to meet to discuss their educational problems in an atmosphere full of honest inquiry and free from pressure, but also because they have only vague ideas of what to do.

When I speak to school audiences, even to whole systems including the school board and the top administrators as I did recently in Fullerton, California, I find that they are receptive to the ideas presented here. Where school systems are willing, as Fullerton was, to close school for a day so that everyone can hear new ideas and then to make definite plans for implementation and follow-up, much can be done. Not only should school close one or two days a year for outside ideas to be presented, but implementation will be most successful when faculty meetings are scheduled as a part of the school week on school time. Because teachers have no more inclination to work overtime than has anyone else, the resentment built by holding meetings after school time will make success for the new programs impossible. Time for faculty meetings can be gained through the use of a minimal school day once a week. (Most states have a minimum time, usually about 4½ hours, that students need to spend in school so that the school can receive state funds. In addition, most schools require teachers to spend at least 7 hours in school. The difference can provide time for faculty meetings. At least 2 hours will then be available for the faculty to meet and to evolve whole-school approaches to implement the philosophy they develop.) Many of the new educational approaches being used in the schools I work in, such as the homogeneous reading group plan described in the previous chapter, have emerged from meetings that I have held with the faculty.

The main innovation that I have introduced in the public schools based on my work at the Ventura School has been the class meeting. Initially, teachers did not think the class meetings were too different from what many of them were already doing. It took many meetings and demonstrations to show the important differences between my approach and the standard school approach to the whole class. (The differences between class meetings and ordinary class discussions will be seen in the next three chapters.) Repeated demonstrations to both entire faculties and to groups of teachers within a school enabled me to convince teachers of the value of the class meetings. If the teachers had not been able to meet with me, we would never have got started. Once teachers start using the class meetings, they need repeated reinforcement through discussion of their progress with this new technique. After a few teachers start holding class meetings based on what they have learned from the discussions and demonstrations, other teachers are encouraged to start so that the meetings can become almost an all-school approach. Children then have an opportunity to participate in class meetings throughout their school years. Teachers appreciate the value of the class meetings when they see children learning to think, listen to others, solve problems, and ponder intellectual questions.

It is not enough just to give the teachers time to meet together. Unless the meetings are well-planned, there will be immediate public reaction against teachers meeting on school time. And unless positive results can be seen to emerge as a result of the meetings, teachers will be vulnerable to charges of wasting time. College classes conducted in the public school can be one type of meeting of teachers that is productive. The classes involve teachers in direct work with the pupils in their classrooms. Many teachers hold provisional certificates and need college courses to obtain a regular credential. Most of them take local college courses little related to their real need: to upgrade their classroom teaching through improving old techniques and learning new ones. Teachers attending classes in the schools who do not need college credits would receive points toward salary increases, a procedure used in Los Angeles (and many other school systems) : I teach a course after school at the 75th Street School sponsored by Mount St. Mary's College. Enrollment has been high (about half the faculty) because the teachers are interested in the subject, classroom discussions. If the class were held on school time as the finish to a minimum day, enrollment would probably be close to 100 percent. Offering the course costs the school system nothing because my salary is paid by Mount St. Mary's. The college benefits by sending regular students to the class who learn from their personal association with experienced teachers. Faculty meetings and college classes in the schools can make a real contribution to improving our schools.

CHAPTER TEN

Classroom Meetings

In this and the following two chapters I shall give a detailed description of the previously introduced classroom meetings, meetings in which the teacher leads a whole class in a non-judgmental discussion about what is important and relevant to them. There are three types of classroom meetings: the *social-problem-solving* meeting, concerned with the students' social behavior in school; the *open-ended* meeting, concerned with intellectually important subjects; and the *educational-diagnostic* meeting, concerned with how well the students understand the concepts of the curriculum. These meetings should be a part of the regular school curriculum. In my experience, they are warmly supported by teachers who agree with the educational philosophy of this book.

Social-Problem-Solving Meetings

The many social problems of school itself, some of which lead to discipline of the students, are best attacked through the use of each class as a problem-solving group with each teacher as the group leader. Teachers in their faculty meetings will do essentially the same thing that each class does in the classroom meeting: *attempt to solve the individual and group educational problems of the class and the school.* When children enter kindergarten, they should discover that each class is a working, problem-solving unit and that each student has both individual and group responsibilities. Responsibility for learning and for behaving so that learning is fostered is shared among the entire class. By discussing group and individual problems, the students and teacher can usually solve their problems within the classroom. If children learn to participate in a problem-solving group when they enter school and continue to do so with a variety of teachers throughout the six years of elementary school, they learn that the world is not a mysterious and sometimes hostile and frightening place where they have little control over what happens to them. They learn rather that, although the world may be difficult and that it may at times appear hostile and mysterious, they can use their brains individually and as a group *to solve the problems of living in their school world.* Over and above the value of learning to solve their problems through class meetings, students also gain in scholastic achievement. This gain is described by Dr. Edmund Gordon, Professor of Psychology and Education at Yeshiva University, in his detailed review of the Coleman Report:*

In addition to the *school* characteristics which were shown to be related to pupil achievement, Coleman found a *pupil* characteristic which appears to have a stronger relationship to achievement than all the school factors combined. *The extent to which a pupil feels he has control over his own destiny is strongly related to achievement.* This feeling of potency is less prevalent among Negro students, but where it is present *"their achievement is higher than that of white pupils who lack that conviction"* (emphasis added).

School children have many social problems, some of which may call for discipline, some not. Under ordinary conditions, because there is no systematic effort to teach them social problem solving, school children find that problems that arise in

* *JACD Bulletin,* Ferkauf Graduate School, Yeshiva University, Vol. III, No. 5, November, 1967.

getting along with each other in school are difficult to solve. Given little help, children tend to evade problems, to lie their way out of situations, to depend upon others to solve their problems, or just to give up. None of these courses of action is good preparation for life. The social-problem-solving meeting can help children learn better ways.

Working with an eighth-grade class of an elementary school, I recently held a social-problem-solving meeting that can serve as an example. Although I do conduct social-problem-solving meetings, they are more difficult for an outsider such as I to hold than for the classroom teacher; students usually feel that someone who doesn't know them well has no business probing into their problems. In terms of Reality Therapy, before one can successfully change behavior, one must be involved. It is difficult for a class and a total stranger to become sufficiently involved with each other to make the meeting successful enough to serve as a demonstration. In contrast, the other kinds of meetings, open-ended and educational-diagnostic, are very easily led by someone the class does not know because these meetings do not present nearly the threat of the social-problem-solving meeting.

A serious problem with the eighth-grade class in the spring of 1967 was truancy. On some of the warmer days, as many as six or eight out of a class of thirty-five would be absent from school. The same children were not absent every day, although some missed school more than others and some always came to class. I was asked to focus on truancy during the meeting. Although no one expected that one meeting would solve such a serious problem, my goals were to get the class to think both about their own motives in cutting school and about some ideas that might help the whole class toward better attendance. The meeting started with my asking the class if everyone were present that day. There was considerable discussion, timid at first but shortly more frank, revealing that about eight students were absent and that those present knew that most of the absentees were not ill that beautiful spring day. When I asked whether some of the students present also frequently skipped class, many admitted that they did. The students sensed that I was nonpunitive and that I was inquiring because I was concerned about their not coming to school.

We discussed at some length what they gained by cutting school and what problems it was causing. We also discussed the school's methods of handling truancy and their parents' reactions to these methods. The students maintained that school was dull and that they saw little sense in what they were learning. They gave the impression that their lives were so full of interesting things to do outside of school that they didn't feel they could attend regularly. They rationalized their position by saying that this year was the last time they would have a chance to cut because next year, when they entered high school, they would have to toe the mark. Questioning their rationale, I said that I doubted that they would attend high school any more regularly. I added that I did not believe that the things they complained about in the eighth grade would be much different in high school. As we continued to talk, most of the students admitted that the reference to high school was rationalization; from their experience with sisters, brothers, and friends, truancy was just as common in high school as in the eighth grade.

At this point we had accomplished what in Reality Therapy would be called exposing the problem for open, honest discussion. My warm and personal attitude helped the class to open up. Talking only about the present problem, we got it out on the table for everyone to examine. Getting this far probably would have been sufficient for the first of a series of meetings aimed at a real solution to the truancy problem. Because the meeting was a demonstration, however, I wanted to go further, and I started pressing the class for a solution. I asked them if they would talk to the absent students to try to get them to stop cutting and to attend school regularly. I knew that unless the students made a value judgment that going to school is worthwhile, they would not attend regularly. It was clear that the statements they made about the value of school were merely lip service. Unless their attitude toward school could be changed, I or anyone else faced an impossible task in trying to get them to come regularly. As was pointed out in Chapter 5, the relevance of the school work must be taught, and where too much irrelevant material is in the curriculum, it must be replaced by material more meaningful to the children.

I attempted, nevertheless, to get from the students present a commitment to attend school the next day. Their wariness toward me and toward anyone who suggested change was apparent in their refusal to make this commitment. The refusal was also a perfect example of the difficulty we have in getting students to participate in irrelevant education. They gave every reason they could think of why they might not be in school the following day. To end the meeting and to help the students understand the importance of making a commitment, I introduced a technique that sometimes works even when a value judgment has not been made: I asked the class to sign a statement promising to come to school the next day. About one-third of the twenty-nine students were willing to sign the statement. The others were very leery about it, giving all kinds of excuses such as that they might be sick or they might be run over on the way to school. They did not want to do anything as binding as signing a piece of paper saying they would attend school. To the nonsigners I said, "If you won't sign a paper stating you will come to school tomorrow, will you sign a paper stating that you won't sign a paper? In other words, will you put your lack of commitment in writing?" After much heated discussion, about one-third more said they would sign the second paper. Although signing this paper did not commit them to come to school, it might still help them to understand the commitment process. One-third of the students remained who refused to sign either paper. I asked them if they would sign a paper stating that they would sign nothing, but they were too smart for me and still refused to sign. I said, "Under these circumstances, will you allow your names to be listed on a piece of paper as students who refuse to commit themselves in any way regarding truancy?" I would put their names on the paper; they would not have participated in the commitment process in any way. To this they agreed, and we obtained the three lists at the end of the meeting.

One meeting with little involvement, no real value judgment, and weak commitment produced, as I expected, no improvement in attendance. There was, however, much discussion not only among these students but also in the entire seventh and eighth grades concerning the class meeting. I had set the stage for a series of meetings to attack the problem of truancy. If this first meeting could have been followed with regular meetings several times a week, the students could have discussed the importance of attending school and been led toward value judgments, plans, and commitments. In class meetings teachers must listen to the reasons given for poor school attendance. When reasons with some validity are given, we must consider changing our teaching to make the school worthwhile to the students where it is not. In addition, we must teach the value of school.

Social-problem-solving meetings such as the one just described are valuable to students and to the school. I suggest that all students in elementary schools wishing to implement the meetings meet regularly during the week for a reasonable time to discuss the problems of the whole class and of individual students within the class. Both students and teachers should consider the class meetings as important as reading, history, or math. The social-problem-solving meetings should be conducted according to the following guidelines that have proved effective both in the public schools and at the Ventura School for Girls, where I first used this technique. Although better guidelines may be developed as the meetings progress, the following should give a good start.

All problems relative to the class as a group and to any individual in the class are eligible for discussion. A problem can be brought up by an individual student about himself or someone else, or by the teacher as she sees a problem occur. In a school with a unified faculty involved with each other and with all school problems, subjects for discussion can be introduced in any class by any student or any teacher, either directly by a note to the group or indirectly by an administrator with knowledge of the problem. In addition to school problems, problems that a child has at home are also eligible for discussion if the child or his parents wish to bring them up.

To adults reading this book, my suggestions may seem strong. As adults, we usually either struggle with our own problems in privacy with little help from friends and family, or we sweep our problems under the rug and try to act as if they don't exist. Thus it may sound as if I am demanding too much of small children. Having held meetings for several years, I have found that children do not think that discussing their problems openly is as difficult as we adults do. The children are concerned because they are learning to deny the existence of their problems. They would much rather try to solve them, and school can give them a chance to do so. Before they come to school, children discover that it is reasonable to try to solve problems. We must be careful, therefore, not to do as we do too often at present: extend our adult anxieties and inadequacies to children and thereby teach them to be evasive as they grow to maturity. In my experience, a class of six-year-olds will freely discuss difficult problems, even one such as stealing (ordinarily a very emotional subject for older children and adults), and try to work out a solution. A solution may require more than just trying directly to get the child to stop stealing, although this of course is the ultimate goal. A solution may include the discovery in the meeting that a child steals because he is lonely, hungry, or jealous, and the working out of ways to correct these causes. Teachers learn during meetings that small children can stand only small temptations. Teachers who do not adequately safeguard lunch money, for instance, are subjecting children to temptation that they may not have the strength to withstand. If children can find a reasonable solution at age six and can concomitantly learn the value of honesty, it is likely that they will never steal again. If someone does steal in a school where discussions are a continuing part of the school program, the stage is set for solving the problem later. The students know that the purpose of all discussion is to solve problems, not to find fault or to punish. Experience in solving social problems in a nonfault-finding, nonpunitive atmosphere gives children confidence in themselves as thinking, worthwhile people.

We have stated that the social-problem-solving meeting is open for any subject that might be important to any child, teacher, or parent related to that class or school. *The discussion itself should always be directed toward solving the problem; the solution should never include punishment or fault finding.* The children and the teacher are oriented from the first meetings in the first grade that the purpose of the meeting is not to find whose fault a problem is or to punish people who have problems and are doing wrong; rather the purpose is to help those who have problems to find better ways to behave. The orientation of the meetings is always positive, always toward a solution. When meetings are conducted in this way, the children learn to think in terms of a solution—the only constructive way to handle any problem—instead of the typical adult way soon learned by school children—fault finding and punishment. The pseudo solution of problems through fault finding is one of the most worthless pursuits continually to occupy all segments of our society. Its constant companion, punishment, is equally ineffective.* Punishment usually works only the first time, if at all. After the first time it works only with successful people, who ordinarily don't need it. Much more often punishment serves as an excuse for not solving a problem rather than leading toward a solution.

It should also be understood that many problems arise that are not readily solvable, that have no single right answer, whose best solution might be a not-so-bad alternative. Sometimes these more difficult problems can be discussed over and over again with little seeming to happen and causing the class and the teacher to become discouraged. A class bully who pushes other children on the playground, dominates the games, and is physically abusive in and out of class often presents such a difficult problem. It seems that the more he is discussed, the less effective the discussion proves to be; the solutions offered by the class work poorly. Even for such a serious problem, the strength of the classroom meetings can be used in two ways. First, often the solution to the problem of such a child lies not so much in coming up with an exact answer, but in the discussion itself. As individual members talk about him, as they see his faults and shortcomings, they become less frightened and less able to be intimidated. Allowing the problem to come out into the open for discussion increases the strength of the bullied students so that gradually, sometimes almost imperceptibly, though the bully's behavior hasn't changed, it becomes less destructive because the others now have more strength. Second, after he is discussed several times, discussion of the bully might be avoided. Unless he does something worthwhile or constructive,

* Two excellent articles support these points. The first, "Whose Fault Was It?," by Charles I. Gragg, *Harvard Business Review*, January–February, 1964, discusses the futility of fault finding. The second is a chapter, pp. 62–67, from *The Human Side of Enterprise*, by John Haberman, McGraw-Hill, 1960. This article deals with an unusual labor-relations program that eliminated punishment completely and that was highly successful. Theoretically, it followed almost exactly the ideas of Reality Therapy as expressed in Chapter 2 of this book.

he is not talked about; if he does something constructive, it is mentioned. This technique removes the attention that he is getting through aggressive behavior and focuses on constructive, positive actions. The teacher might say, "There is no sense talking about Johnny because he is doing the same thing that everyone is complaining about. Let's wait until we can talk about something else he might do that the class would like." Johnny, hearing this and needing attention, will often improve his behavior.

It is important, therefore, in class meetings for the teacher, but not the class, to be nonjudgmental. The class makes judgments and from these judgments works toward positive solutions. The teacher may reflect the class attitude, but she should give opinions sparingly and make sure the class understands that her opinions are not law. Each child learns that he is important to every other child, that what he says is heard by everyone, and that his ideas count. When children experience the satisfaction of thinking and listening to others, they are not afraid to have ideas, to enter into a discussion, and to solve their own problems and the problems of their class by using their brains.

Once an atmosphere of thinking, discussing, and problem solving is established, and it can be established rather quickly, situations that ordinarily would cause serious disturbances in class and that might cause a child to be sent to the principal's office can be handled effectively within the class. Children learn that their peers care about them. They learn to solve the problems of their world. Then it is easy to accept the teacher who says, "We have a problem; these two boys are fighting. At our next class-meeting time we are going to discuss the fight, but now would you boys be willing to stop fighting and wait for the meeting?" This simple request has proved to be effective. The boys stop fighting and wait because they know there is a reasonable alternative to their misbehavior—a solution from the meeting. When they believe that even if they stop fighting they will be punished or expelled from the class, they often continue to fight because the alternatives offered aren't any better than fighting. Classroom meetings can serve to siphon off steam in the class by providing a better alternative. Often the problem is dissipated before the meeting, and the children agree it would be a waste of time to discuss it. The availability of the meeting allowed the children to use the normal ways children have to solve problems.

Meetings should always be conducted with the teacher and all the students seated in a tight circle. This seating arrangement is necessary if good meetings are to occur.

Classroom meetings should be short (10 to 30 minutes) for children in the lower grades and should increase in length (30 to 45 minutes) as the children grow older. The duration of a meeting is less important than its regular occurrence and the pertinence of the problems discussed.

Children who must be excluded from class because their behavior is not tolerable to the teacher or the students will have a better avenue for reentry into the class through the use of class meetings than they have at the present time. Under ordinary school procedures, a principal dealing with a problem child who has been sent out of class finds himself meting out some sort of punishment. He usually swats the child, lectures him, calls in his parents, excludes him from school, or assigns detention time after school or during school. These procedures tend to work less well each time they are applied to any individual child. When the classroom meetings are a part of the school program, the principal has an important added wedge in working with the child. He asks the child sent to his office what he was doing and helps the child understand that *what he did* caused him to be excluded. The principal conducts the discussion with a goal of sending the child back to a class meeting in which the same points will be pursued. The principal counsels the individual child in a way that emphasizes what the child did. In an atmosphere of problem solving instead of punish-

ment, the child usually will discuss his part in whatever happened. The principal then asks the child whether he has any
plan to go back to class. Working with the principal, the child is
asked to make a plan to get back into his class. If he does not
want to go back, he is told that the class will nevertheless try *to
help him* the best they can without him. He is asked to work
out his plan in some detail, which usually does not take much
time. For example, the boy may have been fighting with another boy so much that the teacher finally sends him out of the
class. In a school where he is not threatened with punishment,
he will admit to the principal that he was fighting and, after a
while, admit the part he played in the fight. The principal then
asks him to think about how he could stop fighting. Usually he
says he would do better away from the other boy. This discussion sometimes takes a little time; maybe the other boy has to
come in so that they can agree together on a plan to stay apart
for a while. Both boys take the plan back to the class and the
class may agree to help by not egging them on. In future meetings the class can work on the underlying problem, which may
be jealousy, and the teacher can work on the boys' failure in
school, which usually is a part of behavior problems.

The principal works with the child in a nonpunitive, problem-solving way. Using the class meeting, the child has a built-
in entrée to return to class. As the procedure becomes opera-
tional and the children see that it works, they are happy to use
it because it makes their lives easier. The whole disciplinary
structure of a school should revolve around the class meeting.
Individual discussions with children concerning their problems
should be directed toward individual, and then group-accepted,
solutions.

As time goes on, fewer and fewer disciplinary problems arise,
so that class meetings about behavior disturbances become infrequent. Children learn through problem solving in the group
how to avoid trouble in school and sometimes at home, although it is the rare home where children are encouraged to

solve problems by discussion and planning. If they learn to do so in school, however, the knowledge will prove of value all their lives. Although social-problem-solving meetings often deal with behavior problems, many other subjects can be discussed: friendship, loneliness, vocational choice, and part-time work are examples. The description in Chapter 11 of a series of class meetings and the listing in Chapter 12 of sample questions for meetings both cover many topics for meetings other than behavior problems.

In my experience, much of which has been in schools where discipline was a prime concern, I have found that direct disciplinary meetings are often ineffective in getting children involved with each other in a warm, positive way. They gain *positive involvement* more quickly through meetings in which they discuss ideas relevant to their lives. Earlier in the book I discussed the irrelevance of much of education to the lives of the children in school. I made the point that behavior disorders and educational failure were directly related to this irrelevance. Here it can be shown that classroom meetings, initiated to solve disciplinary problems, can be used effectively to gain and to sustain educational relevance. To understand how this is done, we need to describe two additional kinds of classroom meetings, neither of which directly relates to behavior problems.

Open-Ended Meetings

Probably the cornerstone of relevant education is the open-ended classroom meeting. It is the type of meeting that should be used most often, even where behavior problems are common. When behavior and other social problems are minimal, social-problem-solving meetings will be used infrequently. The open-ended meeting, however, is always applicable; the more it is used, the more relevance can be added to education. In the open-ended meetings the children are asked to discuss any thought-provoking question related to their lives, questions that may also be related to the curriculum of the classroom. The

difference between an open-ended meeting and ordinary class
discussion is that in the former the teacher is specifically not
looking for factual answers. She is trying to stimulate children
to think and to relate what they know to the subject being
discussed.

For example, in meetings with second-grade classes, I have
introduced the subject of blindness. In answer to my question,
"What is interesting to you?" one class said they would like to
talk about eyes and ears. Although the five senses are not a
specific part of the second-grade curriculum, from this introduction an open-ended meeting was held that provided a way
for the students to gain greater motivation to read and to take
more interest in the world around them. In the central-city
school where I first held this discussion, the second graders
usually did not show much intellectual curiosity. What they
didn't know about the world didn't seem to interest them; at
least, it appeared that way. Yet, when an unknown was introduced in a way that made sense to them, they became excited
and showed as much curiosity and as much good thinking as
children who come from more stimulating environments. I
asked the children what they did with their eyes, and they all
said, "See"—a good, simple, factual answer. In a discussion with
small children, it is best to let them begin at a simple level
where they have confidence in their ability to give a good
answer.

Going to a more complex question, I asked, "What do you see
with your eyes?" They mentioned many things, including "the
words in our books." Again they were succeeding in answering a
question; they enjoyed it and were becoming involved. At the
same time, I was able to direct them toward books and reading
in a way new to them. Children are just as stimulated by new
approaches as we are, and they are just as bored with sameness
as we are. One value of the open-ended meeting is to give new
ways a chance to be used. I then asked them about people who
can't see, and they said, "They are blind." A short discussion on

what blindness means followed. Despite an apparent under-standing of blindness, most of the children believed that blind people could really see if they tried hard. We worked at length before everyone understood that blind people could not see at all. The children closed their eyes tight and kept them closed. Slowly, through this participation and discussion, it began to dawn on the class that if you are blind, you cannot see.

By now the children were all involved, but so far they hadn't done much thinking or problem solving. It was important at this time to introduce a problem related to their school work that they could solve if they worked hard. I asked, "Could a blind man read?" The reaction I received from the second graders was laughter, puzzlement, and incredulity. To think that a blind man could read, after they had just confirmed that a blind man couldn't see, was absurd. I asked them to keep think-ing to see if someone could figure out some way that a blind man could read. Of course, I implied that there was an answer. I wouldn't ask second graders a question that had no answer, although in this case the answer was not easy. I insisted that they keep trying to solve the problem; their first reaction when the going got tough was to give up. In school the children had rarely used their brains to solve problems. Accustomed to sim-ple, memorized answers, they gave up when these answers didn't work.

The discussion so far had piqued the children's interest and awakened their faith in their brains. They kept trying, but they were in trouble. The leader must judge when to give them help; he must not do so too soon. I decided to help them at this time by asking if someone would like to take part in a little experiment. We had an immediate raising of hands; they were all eager to help, partly because they sensed that the experiment was a way to keep the discussion going. I selected a boy who, I detected, was not one of the better students or better behaved members of the class. He was waving his hand, eager to volun-teer. Calling him over, I told him to shut his eyes very tight and hold out his hands. I asked him if he were peeking; he said, "No." Putting a quarter in one of his hands and a dollar bill in the other, I asked him if he could tell me what I had put in his hands. The entire class was now glued to the experiment. Some of the brighter students immediately began to glimpse the idea. The boy was able to tell me what was in his hands. I asked him how he knew. Although he wasn't very verbal, he finally said that anyone could tell a dollar bill from a quarter. When I took the dollar bill away and put a nickel in his hand instead, he was still able to distinguish the nickel from the quarter. I then asked him to sit down. Again I asked the class, "How could a blind man read?" Thoughtful students now began to express the idea that if a blind man could feel the letters on a page, he might be able to read. I said, "How could he feel the letters on a page? The page is smooth." And I ran my fingers over a page. One bright child said, "If you took a pin and poked it through the page, you could feel where the pin poked through." From that, most of the class—and they were very excited—was able to get the idea: you could feel the letters on a page!

I still wasn't satisfied, however. I said, "Suppose you *could* feel the letters on the page; I still don't think you could tell one from another." They said they could. I said they couldn't. Suggesting another experiment to try to prove whether or not they could recognize a word by tracing the letters without seeing them, I asked whether they could write their names on the blackboard with their eyes closed. During this discussion I had noticed a little girl sitting next to me trying desperately to follow what was going on. Now she raised her hand vigorously. Every other hand in the class was also raised, but I called on her. Very slowly, somewhat inaccurately although still recognizably, she wrote her name on the board. While she was at the board the teacher, with some alarm, passed me a note saying that the girl was mentally retarded and cautioning me to be prepared for her to fail. Retarded or not, she was fully involved in the experiment. She had managed to scratch something on the board that both she and the class could recognize as her name. Because they were bursting to try, I let some of the other students go to the board to write their names. Most of them did it very well. Through this effort they were able to see the possibility that if they could write their names with their eyes closed, a blind person might feel words in a book. And the smile and eagerness of the "mentally retarded" girl proved that she was as much involved in the discussion as anyone else in the class. Later the class asked what books for the blind look like. They wanted the teacher to bring some in, which she promised to do.

In the discussion after the meeting with the class teacher and several other teachers who were observing, I noted that the meeting could be used as a way to stimulate children to learn to read. The teacher could point out, or have the children point out to her, the advantage of having eyes; reading, difficult as it is for many of these children, is much easier for them than for the blind. The children were deeply involved in the meeting, enjoyed it, and used their brains to think about and solve what seemed at first an insoluble problem. They experienced success as a group and success as individuals. Meetings such as this one in the second grade can be used as motivators in many subjects of the curriculum. In addition, a class that is involved, thinking, and successful will have few disciplinary problems.

In the lower grades, the open-ended meeting may have to be related to the curriculum by the teacher; in the higher grades the class can make the connection. Having a thoughtful, relevant discussion on any subject, however, is more valuable than forcing a connection to the curriculum. In fact, if enough thoughtful discussions are held on subjects not in the curriculum, we should study the curriculum to see where it should be changed.

Educational-Diagnostic Meetings

A third type of class meeting, the educational-diagnostic, is always directly related to what the class is studying. These meetings can be used by the teacher to get a quick evaluation of whether or not teaching procedures in the class are effective. For example, in an eighth-grade class in another school district, I was disappointed to find that the students, despite studying the Constitution for a semester and a half, seemed to know very little about it. Although they had studied its clauses and many of them could recite certain sections from memory, the students had a nonthinking view of the Constitution. Even before the meeting, based on my experience with other classes, I doubted that the students understood the meaning of the Constitution to them as individuals or to the community. To test my opinion, I was given a bright class for the meeting. The questions I asked might be considered unfair by some educators, but we did get a discussion going, and the audience learned that the students had some extremely unconstitutional ideas about the Constitution. Because I had previously complained to the superintendent of schools that the students seemed to have difficulty in handling concepts, I had invited him to join me that day; the meeting I was proposing might pinpoint the difficulty.

My first question to the class was, "What is the Constitution?" The class seemed to be taken aback by this question, but I repeated it several times, adding, "I just want to know if anyone here can tell me what the Constitution is." Looking for some sort of definition or description to start the meeting, I saw immediately that the students were in trouble. It had never occurred to them that anyone would ever ask them what the Constitution is; assuming that everyone, including themselves, knew, they hadn't bothered to think the idea through. The best answer I could get was that the Constitution is something written in books to be studied. I asked them, "Does the Constitution exist? Is there a Constitution on a piece of paper nailed to a wall somewhere that people can see?" The class doubted that it existed in the form I had described. Finally I had to tell them that the Constitution did exist and that people could go to Washington, D.C., and see it. (I usually don't give answers, but I was filled with frustration at this point.)

From this small factual start, I went on to see whether the

students understood the ideas of the Constitution. Following their assurance that they had studied it in detail, I asked them to name some of its important features. When they mentioned the Bill of Rights, I said, "Do these rights pertain to you?" It took some time before they understood what I meant and more time to agree that in fact the Bill of Rights did pertain to the students sitting there. Some of them thought the Bill of Rights did pertain to them, while others thought that it was just for adults. To some extent the latter group was correct because, until the recent Supreme Court decision in the Gault case, minors had almost no protection under the law. Of course they had not learned this in their study of the Constitution.

The key question, however, which brought on a discussion confirming my doubts about the students' understanding of the Constitution, was, "What happens if you do something on your own property that is against the law? For example, may you drive a car on your own property even though you don't have a driver's license and are too young to drive? May you drink a can of beer in your home if your father offers it to you, even though you are legally too young to drink?" I don't know the correct legal answers in these two examples, but that was not the point of the questioning. There was heated discussion. Many of the students suggested that you have no right to break the law on your own property and that you should be punished if you do. I then raised the question of how you could be caught. "Do the police have the right to spy on your house and then come in and arrest you if they think you are drinking beer with your father?" The class said they thought the police did have the right and should do so. I then asked them how the police would know whether a child was having a glass of beer with his father. Although they said that this would be hard to discover, they did have some constructive ideas. One of them was that the police should have a television set focused in everybody's home and, as soon as the police saw anyone doing anything wrong, they should come and get him! Many in the class agreed with this idea and no one disagreed strongly. At that point we dropped the discussion.

It was clear that the discussion was provoking individual thinking about the Constitution. My affirmation of the existence of the Constitution in Washington was the only time during the discussion that I corrected the class or offered them a right answer. In the educational-diagnostic meeting, the leader should not incorporate value judgments into the discussion. The students should feel free to voice their opinions and conclusions in any way they see fit. The teacher learns points of weakness that require additional teaching by her and additional study and discussion by the class. In memory education, where discussions probing understanding rarely occur, students may get answers right on tests and still have no working, living knowledge of something as important as the Constitution and how it pertains to them. Unless the teacher takes a completely nonjudgmental attitude, however, she will never discover these distortions. Cueing to her judgments, students see no reason to discuss their own ideas and opinions.

It is hard for a teacher to conduct an educational-diagnostic meeting because of her involvement with the subject and consequent possible inability to recognize the points that the class may have missed. To see more clearly what a class knows, therefore, teachers might sometimes exchange classes to run these meetings. The blind spots could thereby be eliminated. The educational-diagnostic class meeting should never be used to grade or evaluate the students. It should be used only to find out what students know and what they don't know.

I have described the three kinds of class meetings that I have used during the past several years in my work in the schools. These meetings have proved interesting to students and teachers alike. The technique is not easy for teachers to learn because the required class leadership is not ordinarily taught. Few teachers will conduct meetings without some guidelines, some chance to observe a group, and much approval and encouragement from their superiors. Successful meetings occur only through practice, through evaluating what happens, and through following the guidelines given earlier in the chapter. Unless the meetings are nonjudgmental and open-ended, they will fail.

Enough teachers are conducting class meetings now so that some feedback is available. Many teachers are starting to use some of the techniques involved, especially the circle and the open-ended question, in regular teaching. Going from the open-ended question to some factual material, they encourage students to use judgment and to give opinions. As I write this book, however, most teachers in the schools in which I work have not incorporated classroom meetings into an integral part of their class program. Unfortunately, it is usually isolated from regular teaching. Most teachers conduct meetings one, two, or three times weekly; some report successful, continuing meetings every day. Although some teachers, despite their principal's permission to conduct meetings, still feel guilty about "wasting time" or "playing games," the success of the meetings is slowly winning them over. Students have responded very favorably in every class. Reminding the teacher when a meeting is due, they become involved quickly in the meetings. Because the students don't know that it is hard to have a good meeting, they soon have good meetings, especially in the lower grades. They are eager to participate in discussions relevant to their lives.

When one asks students whether their school work is in any way related to their lives outside of school, most of them reply incredulously, "Of course not." By the tenth grade, students are firmly convinced that school is a totally different experience from life. One learns to live and, completely separately, one learns at school. The three types of class meetings described herein can provide a stable bridge across the gap between school and life.

For the meetings to be most beneficial, they should be used by a majority of the teachers in the school. Children need experience in problem solving and in relating education to life throughout the elementary school period. Learning to think thus builds from year to year. The children gain the important beliefs that they can control their own destinies and that they themselves are a vital part of the world they live in. These beliefs are rarely acquired at present. When I have asked students whether their ideas or interests are important in school, I have been told vehemently in meeting after meeting that, "Our interests have no value in school."

Class meetings keep a class together because the more and less capable students can interact and because students can always succeed. In a meeting, no one can fail. One person's opinion is just as good as another's; there is no right and wrong. The only "wrong," perhaps, is not to participate at all, and this has been a minor problem where meetings are held regularly and with enthusiasm. Overparticipation and talking out of turn are much more common. When, in the open-ended meetings and, to some degree, in the educational-diagnostic meetings, the child succeeds in the eyes of his peers and his teacher, he becomes motivated to do some of the less exciting fact finding necessary to make the judgments and decisions that may evolve from the meetings. If meetings become important and facts become necessary to successful meetings, then it is worthwhile learning facts. The meetings provide the internal stimulus missing from an education that too often starts and ends with facts.

Although I suggest that class meetings be held at a regular time at least once a day in elementary school and perhaps two or three times a week in high school, there is no reason that teachers cannot use the technique for arithmetic, history, science, and other subjects. Whole-class teaching reduces isolation and failure. We use large, cooperative groups in most of the extracurricular subjects. The team, for example, is the basis of competitive athletics. But in the class curriculum, where it could be equally effective, it is little used. By treating the whole class as a unit, the same spirit of cooperation can arise as arises on athletic teams. By eliminating failure, by accepting each child's thinking (at least during the time of the meeting), and by utilizing his mistakes as a basis for future teaching, we have a way of approaching the child that supports him. The present system of accentuating his mistakes tears the child down and makes him unable or unwilling to think.

Another advantage of class meetings is the confidence that a child gains when he states his opinion before a group. In life there are many opportunities to speak for oneself. The more we teach children to speak clearly and thoughtfully, the better we prepare them for life. When a child can speak satisfactorily for himself, he gains a confidence that is hard to shake.

CHAPTER ELEVEN

Getting Meetings Started

Chapter 9 was concerned with the general process of implementing new programs. Here I shall outline the specific steps necessary to implement the classroom meetings. It is unfortunate that the schools are not set up to implement new programs easily, because the way the classroom meetings or any other new program is introduced has a major effect on its success. The principal and the school counselor should take the main responsibility to introduce classroom group meetings into a school. Even if the counselor is part-time, as he usually is in elementary schools, he should devote a part of that time to help implement the new program. In Chapter 9, I discussed the need for the principal to organize the faculty into a working, problem-solving group. The principal can use the help and the skills of the guidance counselor. Together they can work to organize constructive faculty meetings.

Although the principal's role in a school is rather clearly understood, the role of the guidance counselor is less well understood by parents, teachers, and children. Ordinarily, we think of a guidance counselor as one who works with individual problem students and helps them to solve their problems, much as a psychologist or a psychiatrist might work in his office with a patient. Some satisfactory counseling is done this way, but the time required for the many children with problems far exceeds the time that hard-pressed guidance counselors have to offer to individual children. Guidance counselors also work with teachers and parents to help them deal more effectively with children. This work naturally varies from school to school and from counselor to counselor. In most schools, contacts between the guidance counselor and the classroom teachers that are beneficial to both rarely occur. Part of the problem arises from the mechanics of the situation. Working with students at the same time, they have little chance to talk to each other.

The role of the guidance counselor is, however, the main reason for the poor relationship between counselor and teacher. The counselor receives a referral from a teacher, tests the student extensively, writes a report based on the test results, and submits the report to the teacher. Both guidance counselors and teachers are unhappy with this often meaningless procedure based upon the unsound idea that tests will point out areas where children can be helped. What tests actually do is convert the teacher's observation of what is wrong with the child into the jargon of psychological diagnosis. The teacher will say the child seems withdrawn and timid; the guidance counselor, after testing, will report that the child is a borderline schizophrenic. This description does not help the teacher. Instead, it frightens her and makes her feel that she is dealing with a serious psychological problem for which she has had no training. When, as is often the case, the guidance counselor can offer no help for the child, either because he is too busy or because the child is an extremely difficult case to work with, the teacher becomes skeptical of the value of the referral procedure. Because the referral procedure is traditional, however, few people have seriously questioned its value.

Guidance counselors, except for those few who are most limited and least perceptive, are unhappy with their roles as psychometric diagnosticians. Teachers are unhappy because they are unable to use the material the guidance counselor obtains. Principals often rise above the whole procedure by paying little or no attention to it. Rather than continue the ineffective referral and testing procedure, tests, except in rare and well-defined cases, should be abandoned.The guidance counselor should learn more about group processes and then work directly in classes demonstrating to classroom teachers how to deal with their classes effectively as counseling groups. Although most guidance counselors haven't the skill to do this at the present time, they have the educational and professional background to take group-counseling courses which, while not exactly applicable, do provide some help in learning to conduct class meetings. Counselors are usually more interested in learning group work (and they have more time to do so) than the average principal. A counselor could still work with individual children when he is urgently needed. He would, however, stop devoting most of his time to the traditional but meaningless procedure of testing and instead go into the classroom to help the classroom teacher learn to conduct class meetings effectively.

Before a guidance counselor could spend time in the classroom helping teachers, he would need the permission and cooperation of the school superintendent and the principals of the schools in which he worked. It goes without saying that new programs cannot be implemented without full support from the top. One of the reasons for writing this book is to obtain this support. Working in the schools as a consultant psychiatrist, a role similar to that of the guidance counselor, I have, with administrative support, implemented the class-meeting program in the following ways. Nothing I have done is outside the traditional school structure. Everything can be accomplished during the time of the average school day.

As described in Chapter 9, first it is necessary to hold a meeting of the teachers in which the principal, with my help or the help of the guidance counselor, explains to the faculty the purposes of the program. During the meeting, reference can be made to other group work being done in the schools. Time is available for answering questions and for discussion. As teachers show interest, they are invited to join voluntarily in a pilot program. Attempts to go too fast, or to pressure teachers into adopting a program whose value they doubt, will serve no purpose. As part of the introductory process, class meetings are demonstrated in classrooms or in the auditorium in front of the faculty. Demonstration meetings that I have conducted have aroused much interest. Teachers must see classes involved in discussion to understand the procedure and how it works. When teachers see how capable their students are during a demonstration meeting, they become interested and excited. Trying to conduct meetings themselves, however, they often find it difficult.

It is important to stress the difficulty of what looks so simple when someone with experience does it, and to explain to teachers that they should not be discouraged if they don't get good meetings from the start. In my work with the schools, I demonstrate three or four meetings a day to different groups of teachers. It is best to demonstrate with the same classes from week to week for five to ten weeks so the teachers can see progress. Sometimes the meetings are very effective, sometimes they fall flat. I was very nervous when I started to do these demonstrations because I was concerned that, if the meetings went poorly, the teachers would feel they were not worthwhile. I was surprised after one poor meeting when several teachers came up to me and said, "That was great! That's what happens to me!" Instead of causing them to lose interest, the poor meeting reassured them that leading a class meeting is difficult and that even experienced leaders fail. My belief that each demonstration meeting had to be perfect may have, for many teachers, done just the opposite of what I had intended; that is, I made the teachers think that the procedure was too hard when they didn't get similar results. Learning to conduct class meetings takes practice, just as learning to do anything else does. The class learns as well as the teacher. There are good meetings and bad ones. Teachers shouldn't be discouraged or give up because things don't work out to their expectations from the beginning. This point cannot be stressed enough. Teachers as well as students are not encouraged by failure. If we expect students to work to understand and implement new ideas, we must not be afraid to do the same.

After a teacher sees the demonstration meetings and expresses interest, the principal or counselor goes to her class to work with her to get the meetings started. For the principal to be effective in assisting teachers, they must be comfortable with each other, an uncommon situation in most schools. The faculty meetings suggested in Chapter 9 can help principals and teachers to be able to work together without strain. A teacher need not be uneasy when the principal comes into her class and attempts to help her get meetings started, because conducting meetings is not a skill that the teacher is expected to know. The principal can say that he has had little experience in developing the skill himself. Now the teacher and principal are on common but unfamiliar ground; in a sense they are partners in a strange land. The development of the skills to run the meetings can be used to become comfortable working together. In addition, working together breaks down the artificial barrier between teacher and principal with regard to the teacher's classroom performance.

The summary of a series of social-problem-solving meetings follows. The principal conducted the meetings at first, with the teacher watching. Later, the teacher took over and ran the meeting herself.

We met in the fourth-grade class for the first time on February 23 from 11:20 to 12:00 and every Thursday at the same time until the end of the term. There were about 17 class meetings. I [the principal] did about 10 or 11 and Miss Allen the rest.

We both feel that the changes in attitude and behavior were phenomenal. This was a group of 37 (19 boys, 18 girls) nine- to ten-year-olds. While it included many individually capable and wonderful children, their class feeling was pretty much "dog eat dog!" They had developed fairly complex skills of putting each other down, and the children they "respected" were high-handed and bullying in their leadership. What seemed to turn the tide, I think, was feedback from the class to John, who was the class leader. He expressed surprise and dismay that other children were hurt and unhappy about the way he treated them. At this point, John and I had some one-to-one talks and he was wholeheartedly willing to use his leadership in a constructive way. He became instrumental in class meetings in creating a climate of frankness and honesty. He would not let the others get away with alibis for their behavior. And because he was serious, even passionate about expressing his opinions, the meetings became vital and exciting.

I'm hoping the meetings will take hold throughout the school in September. I have found the discussions a powerful, effective instrument for changing group behavior; the absence of punishment (which includes "nagging") has made it possible to keep a fascinating dialogue going and creates a much happier, open relationship between children and teacher.

The principal also asked the teacher for her comments on what went on in her class. Following is her report:

Evaluation of the class at the beginning of the term:
Very bright, anxious children, eager to learn and with a wide background of experiences. However, much tension in intergroup relationships, very little willingness to "give" or bend, much selfishness displayed, and an eagerness to "get ahead" at the expense of others. Much tattling and an eagerness to get others in trouble. Seemed to be a group who could hardly work together.

Some brief descriptions of what happened at some of the class meetings:
The question was asked, "How many think this is a kind class?" About eight boys thought that it was. Those who did were the boys who were mostly unkind themselves, except for two. The class then gave the opinion that these boys themselves were not kind boys. It was true that especially John (the leader of the dissident group) and Bill (his cohort) had often done cruel things to

others. They took great pleasure in ambushing and beating up Mike, making remarks of a very cutting nature to most of the other children, hiding articles belonging to others, stealing money, leaving school early, and blurting out negative opinions in class at will (this last being a problem of John, not Bill). The boys in question were quite shocked that the others held such an opinion of them, and appeared a little shaken. Their own self-images seemed to be a bit different from that of their peers. The class discussed the difference between humor which was funny and that which was cruel. They talked about what it feels like inside when a person laughs at the expense of others, how it hurts. This led to another topic, what feels good in a relationship and what feels bad, a topic which we discussed the next time. Before ending this meeting, David wanted to know why the class had not let it be known if he was a kind person. It was explained to him that he had not been one to say he felt it was a kind class. He wanted to know anyway, and was happily shocked to see they felt he was a kind person. He had mixed it up with whether they liked him or not, and beamed when he received this vote of confidence. He said he always felt no one liked him before, and that he was an outsider.

Joanne opened another meeting with the topic of friendship. She was new to the school and felt she had no friends in the class. The children discussed what had happened to them when they had been new to the school that made them feel good. Harriet and Ann told how they had approached Carol when she first came to school and Carol told what a warm glow she experienced from their attempts at friendliness. The children also discussed what had sometimes happened to them that made them feel bad. They seemed to agree that careful explanations of rules and practices without getting mad at a new person was most important. They also talked about what characteristics a friend has. Jerry felt it was someone who didn't tattle on you when you did something bad. The other children let it be known that this in the long run hinders the friend if he is in need of guidance, rather than helps him. (The example he cited was hitting the driver of a passing truck with his BB gun and another boy seeing it but not reporting him.) It turned out that Joanne's problem was much caused by her own actions, which the others called "being spoiled," and that she did not try to adjust or conform to their standards of behavior or rules. Helen patiently explained to her that they were trying very hard, but that it requires give and take on both sides and that she really wasn't trying her hardest to be fair. Raye, who also was exasperated with Joanne, was less patient. The girls agreed to try much harder and were made very much aware of Joanne's problems and feelings. However, as the semester progressed, the others reached their frustration level and felt like giving up with Joanne, who reportedly was not trying at all to cooperate.

At another meeting, Mike was introduced as the topic. Physically overweight and not too clean-looking in appearance, with hair in his eyes and a very loud, offensive voice, and holes in all his tee shirts caused from biting and twisting and chewing on them, he was not pleasant to behold! Mike said he didn't like the class because they didn't like him. When asked why they didn't like him, he said it was because he was fat. The children eagerly disagreed. They said that had nothing to do with it. Mike wanted to know why, then. He was given the opportunity to call on those children he wanted to explain to him what they found offensive about him. Someone said it was because he wears funny hats to school, like the pilot's helmet he wore the day before. (Incidentally, he never wore it again.) Some said he dressed sloppily. Martin said it was because he said things that hurt people. For example, when Martin came home from Europe and showed the class several treasures that he brought to share, Mike said he didn't believe they were from Paris and that he bought the same things here. Martin said that hurt his feelings. David said that when he shared things with the class, Mike blurted out similar derogatory remarks. (Mike still has not cured himself of this, by the way.) John, who had become much more introspective and perceptive, said it was because Mike always made funny faces and looked up at the ceiling with a disgusted look on his face when people tried to talk to him. While he was saying this, Mike was doing just that. John said, "See, Mike, you're doing it right now, and you don't even know it." Mike was asked if anyone, in his opinion, went out of his way to be nice to him. He said, only Alice, whom he liked. Everyone giggled. Alice said she didn't care if everyone did laugh at her, she liked Mike and was not ashamed to be his friend. She liked being nice to him. We talked as a group about the importance of having one friend at least. The others found that no one really tried to go out of his way to be his friend, but each person would try to make some gesture to show they would try in the next week. They really rose to the occasion, but soon forgot about it and were their usual apathetic selves. However, no one seemed to go out of his way to be nasty, which was a change. Alice continued being nice to Mike, and the children stopped teasing her about it. Harriet, who was one of the girls who was teasing Alice, apologized in a class meeting for doing so, and she said she had once been teased for befriending someone without other friends, and that it took more courage to be his friend and yet she wanted to. She told Alice that, even though it had hurt her feelings when the others teased her, she had forgotten and teased Alice and that she was sorry, as she could really understand how Alice felt. There has been a tremendous change in Mike this semester. He is not lackadaisical about his work or appearance, speaks more quietly, uses more self control, plays a fairer game in the yard, gets along much better with others, and has more (or some) friends.

Joe was brought up at another meeting, because he follows around the noon-aides. He said he doesn't like to play the games because at his old school they were played differently. The team explained that even though he wasn't a good player, they still needed him and his absence made the teams unequal. The children agreed to tell him kindly their rules, and he promised to make an effort to be always present. It solved itself in this way.

As the class saw their individual and class problems working out, they tried to solve bigger problems. They said that, in the yard, balls from other areas are kicked to opposite ends of the playground instead of being returned to the area from where they came, thus delaying and spoiling the game. The girls felt that kindness would be repaid with kindness, and that if a ball came to their area and was handed back to the owner, it would be remembered next time their ball went into a strange area, and then their ball would be handed back rather than be kicked away. The boys said it would never work, and that the older children would still get pleasure out of kicking the ball away no matter how many times they handed theirs back. They suggested I talk with the other teachers and some kind of rule be made that this was not proper behavior. Older children who continued to kick the younger children's ball would be excluded from that area until they were willing to stop. This is what actually happened, and games are now more pleasurable, at least in that respect.

In one of the last meetings, we discussed hurt feelings due to unfairness of certain team captains. We talked about what a team captain should be like and which boys had been good examples of team captains. The children who were not the skilled players felt that they should get some good positions occasionally, instead of being out in the field all the time. They said the only way they could get to be better players is to be allowed to try or practice in some of the choice positions. Bill said he tries to give everyone a chance, sometimes in some choice positions, and the others agreed he was pretty fair. The good players complained that if the poor players held key positions, the team would never win, so a good team captain should keep this in mind. They felt Sam did a good job of keeping this objective in mind without always monopolizing certain positions with certain players. Sue's team felt she was a good captain because she never gave positions to people who begged for them. Paul, a good player, was told by the others that if the umpire or rules say someone is "out," whether he agrees or not, he should hold his temper. When he was a team captain he had certain authority, and now that he isn't, he should respect the authority of the team captain elected.

Evaluation of the class at the end of the term:

Great improvement in ability to explore what it is that is bothering them and to express their hostility and anger by communicating with their peers and looking for a solution collectively, rather than to tattle or be interested in revenge as their main goal in any hurtful situation. Attitudes toward others of a much more understanding nature. Deeply influenced by peer acceptance and feelings, much more so than that of adults in authority. The absence of serious punitive measures for telling about things they had done or were doing let the air be cleared and consciences eased, and peer reaction seemed to influence their future behavior in this area. Leadership ability that had been channeled negatively was shown to be a great asset to the group when channeled positively. All in all, the class became more perceptive and willing to help one another.

In other schools, where the principals are in my class, similar results have been obtained during the first year that class meetings have been held. Teachers from these schools have come to observe my demonstrations both during the day at the 75th Street School and in the evenings (on their own time) at various schools. The enthusiasm of the principals in my class for class meetings is perhaps both cause and effect of the excellent results that many of their teachers are getting through using them. At Miramonte, an 1800-student elementary school near the 75th Street School, the teachers themselves have organized a study group led by a teacher who is a member of my class. Her principal and superintendent were able to get salary point credit for this class. Attendance has been excellent. Many teachers at Miramonte have been implementing the class meetings in their own rooms based upon a few demonstrations and a lot of conviction that the meetings are worthwhile. In the several districts of the Los Angeles city school system in which I have worked, there has been good support by the superintendents. I believe that the program will expand considerably over the next four or five years.

I shall restate here the procedures required to initiate and maintain class meetings:

1. The educational philosophy outlined in the earlier chapters of this book is discussed by the school faculty. In my experience, agreement is usually reached among the teachers, the administrators, and the counselors that the class meetings are a possible solution to some of the educational problems so prevalent in the school.

2. If at all possible, a teacher, counselor, or principal who has had some experience in working with a class in each of the three types of meetings demonstrates meetings to individual teachers and to the whole faculty. If no one in the school has had direct training, the principal or counselor must try to learn to conduct

meetings on his own and take the initial responsibility. To do so, the principal or counselor works with the classes of one or two interested teachers and then uses these classes for demonstrations. A teacher who is trained and willing to demonstrate her skill to other teachers will help the program to expand more rapidly than if all demonstrations are done by the principal or counselor.

3. I have tried meetings using almost every type of seating arrangement available in a class. The large-circle arrangement, with the teacher and the class sitting in a single circle, is by far the most effective. With any other seating arrangement, some children cannot see or hear each other. It is then almost impossible to establish communication and hold a successful meeting. Having had successful meetings, many teachers change the arrangement of their classes from the traditional rows for regular teaching. They find the children so responsive in the circle that they approximate this arrangement for all teaching by arranging the desks and chairs in a U. Then they need only fill in the top of the U to make a meeting circle. There is then little disorganization in getting from the classroom seating to the meeting circle. Teachers have also found that, if the chairs are arranged in the circle while the children are on the playground during recess or lunch, there is less confusion. Many teachers have appointed monitors to arrange the chairs during these times. This job is excellent for a child who ordinarily doesn't participate well in the meeting because it makes him feel that he is an important part of the process.

4. The teacher sits in a different place in the circle each day. In addition, she makes a systematic effort to arrange the children so that the meeting will be most productive. Boys who squirm and nudge one another can be separated. Boys and girls are interspersed, as are the vocal and the quiet children. Sometimes the teacher sits next to children who tend to disturb the meeting so that she can restrain them. Sometimes she sits next to children who are uncommunicative because her presence

often encourages them to talk. Some children, however, will not talk when they sit next to the teacher; she must move often enough to ensure that she does not inhibit these children.

Children welcome visitors to the meetings. Visitors, who usually stimulate and improve meetings, always sit in the circle with the children and are encouraged to participate as regular members of the group. The teacher can decide the number and the kinds of visitors. As meetings continue, both children and teachers from other classes are encouraged to come as visitors. The principal is a regular visitor at various meetings throughout the school year.

5. In learning to conduct meetings, it is good for teachers to team. Provision is made to relieve a teacher so that she can attend a meeting in her team teacher's class. The team teachers should have equal opportunity to attend meetings in each other's class. They should then have an opportunity to discuss their progress, both in regular faculty meetings after school and informally as time permits. During the meeting, the team teacher can be either an observer, perhaps taking notes that are used as a basis for later discussion, or a coleader. Teachers are teamed voluntarily; usually good friends among the faculty make good teams. The teams should be shifted periodically, however, so that interested teachers have an opportunity to work with several other teachers.

6. Subjects for open-ended discussion may be introduced by the teacher, as she sees fit, or by the class. The teacher encourages the class to think of relevant subjects. Sometimes she may allow the students to start the meeting and then shift to a subject that she would like them to discuss. For example, an important subject to be discussed in school is the problems of democracy. The teacher can begin by asking the class what they would like to talk about. If they mention some entertainment facility, as they often do (Disneyland being popular near Los Angeles), the teacher can translate the mention of Disneyland into an actual democratic, problem-solving process by asking, "Who

would like to go to Disneyland?" Almost every child will want
to go. The teacher may then say, "Suppose someone gave me
two tickets to Disneyland and said I should give these tickets to
two children in my class. To whom should I give the tickets?"

In the many times that I have used this question as a basis for
discussion in second- through sixth-grade classes, the discussion
has always been heated. The children are vitally concerned with
deciding fairly and democratically. The final solutions have
ranged from the class getting together and earning money so
that everyone, not just two, could go, to giving the tickets away
because the class could not make a democratic, thoughtful decision. The latter solution is very infrequent. The most frequent solution is to select two students, one good and one poor,
who have never been to Disneyland. The students' reasoning is
that good effort should pay off, but that in school it pays off too
much. Those who do badly get nothing and have little incentive
to do better. The children believe that a trip to Disneyland
would give the less successful student incentive to do better in
school. They also say that the good students and the poor students rarely associate; getting together for a pleasant afternoon
at Disneyland would be beneficial to both. Few adult groups
could equal this application of democracy. Once a teacher gets
the feel of the meetings, she becomes skilled in shifting a class-
suggested topic to a thoughtful, open-ended question.

7. Disciplinary meetings should not be repetitive. Discussing
a problem child day after day does more harm than good.* Open-
ended and educational-diagnostic discussions that are interesting enough to attract the participation of the problem children

---

* This is illustrated by the charming note sent to a principal who had been
having meetings:

Dear Miss Allen:
Could we please stop discussing Joanne's prombles at the class
meetings. The class is getting *tired* of her prombles!!!

Your Friend,
Marianne M., Room 10

lead to improved behavior. On the other hand, when important disciplinary problems arise, there should be no reluctance to name names and bring the difficulty out into the open in the class meetings. One meeting leads to another; often problems brought up in Monday's meeting and barely touched upon can form the basis for meetings the rest of the week.

8. Meeting duration should depend upon the age and meeting experience of the class. In the beginning primary-grade children find it difficult to maintain attention for more than 10 or 15 minutes. The time can usually be worked up to 30 minutes, a good meeting length. Fourth, fifth, and sixth graders can meet for 30 minutes or longer and hold interesting discussions. In my experience, holding the meetings to a specific duration is better than allowing meetings to vary in time from day to day. Thus teachers should feel free to cut off a meeting, even during a hot discussion, and tell the students that they are at a good place to start the next meeting. The meeting should not be allowed to drag overtime and become an excuse for the children to avoid other responsibilities during the day. Sometimes, however, especially during disciplinary meetings, it is necessary to extend the meeting a little to allow time to work out a beginning solution.

With primary-grade children, meetings are more effective if they are held before recess, before lunch, or before the school's closing time. These times both provide a natural cutoff for the meeting and allow the interesting meeting to fill a time in the day when children's attention normally lags.

I believe that meetings should be held daily and at a regularly scheduled time. Once a week is the minimum frequency; meeting less often than that does not provide enough continuity in the discussions. Thus one to five meetings a week are the minimum number necessary for the program to be effective.

9. Children seem to respond best if they are given an opportunity to raise their hands. Some teachers are able to run meetings in which children politely wait for an opportunity to talk

without hand raising. This desirable goal is difficult to reach. Because I have never been able to work with a group long enough to attain it, I rely upon hand raising. In calling on children who raise their hands, it is not necessary to be completely democratic. Certain children are going to contribute to a discussion and keep it going; others are not. Part of the skill of running a meeting is learning when and when not to call on different children.

Many children who do not seem able or willing to raise their hands are listening actively and have much to say. It is all right for the leader to call on these children, usually with a remark such as, "You have been listening very carefully; I wonder if you would like to contribute something?"; or, "I'm sure you have an idea about this, and I would like to hear from you." Positive, supportive remarks such as these often lead a child who will not raise his hand to participate. Not insisting if the child declines to speak at first, the teacher should add, "I'm sure you will have something to say in a little while; I'll come back to you then." Very often when I have said this, the child's hand is waving in the air in a few moments. As soon as possible I try to give him a chance to speak. Ordinarily, however, participation is not a problem once the children become accustomed to the meetings.

Some teachers at the 75th Street School have succeeded in getting the children to speak without raising their hands. They take turns politely and talk to each other rather than the teacher. Working with their classes in demonstration meetings has been very exciting for me. These teachers have gone beyond what I have been able to accomplish in my demonstrations. Their success shows how much can be accomplished in class meetings by interested teachers and the resultant involved students.

10. A teacher never interrupts a child to correct bad grammar, bad usage, or mild profanity. These interruptions are destructive. A child corrected when he is desperately struggling to

express an idea or use his brain to solve a problem is so put
down that he may never volunteer again. He may then become
uninterested and disruptive during the meetings.

Sometimes a child will talk endlessly on a subject that interests him but that bores the class. This situation is handled by
the teacher intervening after a reasonable period of time and
saying, "We would like to go on to someone else; we'll come
back to you in a little while," or some statement to that effect. If
it is done properly, the child will not be put down.

11. Children will often become very personal, talking about
subjects that ordinarily are considered private. These may include activities both at home or in their neighborhood. In this
situation the teacher should keep in mind that in the class meetings free discussion seems to be beneficial and that adult anxieties are often excessive. Nevertheless, a child who discusses
drunken brawls at home might be quietly asked to talk about
something that has more relationship to school. Changing the
subject in this way is sometimes unwise, however, because it is
just those drunken brawls at home that have the most relationship to his school progress.

In my experience, if we follow the guidelines given for class
meetings, children rarely lapse into fantasy or lie. When flights
of fantasy do occur, the teacher can simply call on someone else.
When the teacher does suspect lying, she can ask the class
whether or not they believe the child is telling the truth. The
class, not the teacher, should judge. If enough meetings are
held, the truth eventually comes to the surface; lying is best
combated by holding meetings regularly and often.

Class meetings work as well as the imagination, ingenuity,
and conviction of those who run them. They will not, however,
take the place of other educational changes needed and described in Chapters 3 through 8.

CHAPTER TWELVE

Keeping the Class Meetings Going

Many more new programs are started than become established in the schools. They fail for a variety of reasons, the most important of which is that the teachers don't feel that the program is of value. Or if they do feel it is of value, they don't understand how to use it, they don't succeed with it, and they quit. Teachers withstand failure no better than students do. If they don't succeed quickly with a new program, they stop. Conducting class meetings, a technique that few teachers have been prepared for either by their own experience as students or by their training, often meets great resistance from teachers.

Teachers who work hard enough to get successful meetings going are enthusiastic about them. The meetings are enjoyable for everyone, and the students also become enthusiastic. Many teachers meet regularly, some every day. At the 75th Street School, use of the class meetings has produced remarkable involvement for children in classes that have had regular meetings. The children display tolerance, maturity, and thoughtfulness. They have learned to care for each other. As the meetings progress successfully, the teachers have learned to be at ease. They see that the particular questions they raise are not crucial to the meeting's success because the students will carry the meeting once they get used to the process. Most of all, they have not become discouraged if the meetings are not good every day. Convinced that the meetings are valuable even though their results cannot be measured objectively, they take pleasure in seeing their poorer students respond well for the first time. When the meetings reduce behavior problems, increase educational motivation among uninterested students, and provide a vehicle for bringing relevance into education, they make these discussions a regular part of their daily program.

For every teacher who gets a class discussion going, there is at least one other teacher who believes in the method, who has tried it and would like to continue, but who falters because she cannot think of enough questions that lead to interesting meetings. Teachers who depend too much in the beginning on the class to suggest discussion subjects become discouraged when they find that the class cannot do so. When the teacher, as well as the class, runs out of questions, the teacher reduces the number of meetings and breaks the regular meeting pattern. Once this pattern is broken, the meetings become much less valuable.

In this chapter I shall explain how a leader arrives at questions that lead to interesting meetings, discuss the merits of various questions, and develop several series of questions for class meetings. Thinking of good questions is a part of good teaching; the inability to think of good questions is symptomatic of the fact-centered education that we must change. Holding class discussions should be within the reach of any teacher who tries to understand her students and their interests. A continuous flow of new questions that are relevant and stimulating can be developed from the discussions. I have found that most teachers can eventually learn to keep meetings going but, because the technique is new, they ask for help in thinking of questions to get started.

When a teacher initially develops what she believes is a good question, she often finds, to her discouragement, that the class does not react as she had expected. What seems interesting to her does not interest the class, a discovery that a thoughtful teacher can use to increase her teaching effectiveness. Even when she poses a good question, a question that interests and stimulates the class, she may lack the skill to develop the question to the point where the students become intensely involved. It is not enough, therefore, to arrive at a good initial question. Also required is good development of the subject through a series of following questions. During the development period, the teacher must be flexible, sense the mood or interest of the class, and rephrase and rework the question to fit that mood or interest. If she does not succeed on one particular day, no harm is done. She should try again the next day and the next. Classes are tolerant of teachers attempting to get class meetings started because they recognize their value. No teacher need feel uncomfortable if she can't phrase and develop good questions immediately. If a teacher believes enough in the value of the meetings to keep them going for a semester despite some poor meetings, she will almost certainly attain the skill to lead good meetings. If, after three or four meetings, she runs out of good questions, becomes discouraged, reduces the frequency of meetings, and begins to hold them at irregular intervals, she will not have spent enough time to learn to lead meetings successfully. The meetings will falter and stop.

Teachers must understand that, when students are asked to think and participate in discussions, a new experience for most of them, they are unprepared and therefore hesitant to speak their minds. In the beginning, a few of the so-called good students, who would rather do the rote memory and fact work of ordinary education, resist. Although they are willing to speak when they know the answer in a regular class quiz session, they hesitate at first when open-ended meeting questions are posed. The poor students find that, when they don't respond in the usual class question-and-answer periods, the teacher stops calling on them. They drop out and let the memorizers carry the class. The thinking questions asked during class meetings often stimulate poor students to respond, but students who have stopped thinking for too long still do not participate. With a class of intellectual dropouts, even the best leader may find it impossible to stimulate a thoughtful discussion, a common situation in junior and senior high schools. Some junior college teachers have complained to me that the students in their classes refuse to enter into discussions, even in specifically formed discussion groups of fifteen to twenty-five. The students ask if the discussion topics are going to be on the test and, if they are not (and in most cases they are not because objective tests are usually used), they are not interested. They want to spend their time learning the right answers for the tests; with the present undue emphasis on grades, it is hard to blame them. The teachers tell me that discussing the subject intellectually, getting to the core of the argument, and asking interesting questions are of little interest to their students. Their refusal to participate in discussions indicates a kind of intellectual atrophy, similar to what happens to an arm or a leg when it is immobilized for a long time in a plaster cast for the healing of a broken bone. With the intellect, as with an arm or leg, exercise is needed to prevent atrophy. Throughout the school years, class meetings can provide the exercise needed to be able to participate in thoughtful discussions.

As many teachers know and can easily demonstrate, most children in the first several grades of school are willing to participate in an intellectual discussion. Little children will think and talk. We must encourage them to do so by listening to them and by teaching others in the class to listen also. It is easier and more effective to start these discussions in kindergarten than to try to start them in later grades. When children learn to express themselves thoughtfully and without fear, when they learn to listen and to take an interest in what others have to say, they have developed a skill that probably correlates with success in life more than anything else taught in school.

In working with students of all ages, I have repeatedly found that general questions provide little stimulation. It takes a long time and many meetings before students are ready to tackle generalities. For example, "Why do we go to school?" may seem to be a good question. Instead of being stimulated however, the students answer with clichés. The discussion becomes an impersonal, rote exercise in which they mouth the answers they believe the teacher wants to hear, such as,

"A good education leads to a good job."
"Education is important for college."
"Education is important for life."

They continue these clichés, never getting to the meat of what going to school is all about. If we change the question by giving it a catch such as,

"If each of you could have a million dollars right now, a sum that would be ample for the rest of your life, would you continue to go to school?"

This more pointed question has produced great food for thought. Many students say they wouldn't go to school, others say they would. I ask those who say they wouldn't,

"What would you do with your life?"

I ask them specifically what their plans would be and whether they think that carrying out their plans would be enjoyable and productive. I push them past nervous, joking responses such as,

"Just eat candy."
"Watch TV."
"Go to ball games."

These joking responses are defenses against their anxiety because they are intelligent enough to understand that they need to go to school. I then ask both those who say that they would continue to go to school and those who say they wouldn't,

"Why would you go to school? Just a few minutes ago you said that the purpose of education was to get a good job. Now you say you would continue to go to school even if you didn't need the money from a job."

To develop a series of questions relating to education and a job, we may discuss the value of a good job beyond the financial reward, using the following questions:

> *"If you still want to go to school to get a good job, even though you would have enough money, work must be important. Why is work important? And if work is important, how does education relate to work? Is it important for you to be occupied instead of just sitting around your house or just looking for fun for the rest of your life?"*

I may try to get an argument going between the two groups of children, those who would quit school now because they have the million dollars and those who would continue going to school and later go to work. I spice the discussion with questions such as,

> *"Do all rich men's sons avoid work?"*
> *"Why, in many cases, do rich men work harder than people who are poor?"*

The discussion may eventually lead from riches to poverty as I ask about poor people who do not work hard. The following questions may carry the idea further:

> *"Do some poor people work as hard or even harder than rich people?"*
> *"What are the differences between poor people and rich people?"*
> *"Are these differences big?"*
> *"Are these differences important?"*
> *"In what ways are the rich and the poor the same?"*
> *"Have any of you ever known a poor person?"*
> *"What was he like?"*
> *"Have any of you ever known a rich person?"*
> *"What was he like?"*

Further questions may then follow:

> *"How does the government make sure that poor people get enough money to live on?"*
>
> *"Do you understand what government welfare programs are?"*
>
> *"Do you understand why these programs are necessary?"*
>
> *"Are there better ways of helping people who can't support themselves than putting them on government welfare?"*
>
> *"Do people really want this kind of a life for themselves?"*
>
> *"How do people apply for welfare?"*
>
> *"How do poor people get along who can't get welfare?"*

From the initial subject of "Why do you go to school," we discussed the subjects of work, poverty, and welfare, a good example of how one general question can be developed intensively, made more specific, and then moved through several associated topics. Discussions such as this can be extended for several sessions, even weeks, with an interested class. When the students come from homes where newspapers, magazines, and books are available, they can be encouraged to read them to help bring current ideas to the discussion. Children from lower-income families can ask their parents, who are often by circumstance well-qualified to answer, about these subjects. The parent would necessarily become involved with his children on a subject that is understandable, relevant, and important to the family.

We have already discussed that most students will still go to school even if they had enough money so that they would never have to work. We haven't discussed what they might learn in school under these circumstances.

> *"If you had enough money so that you didn't have to go to school to prepare you to earn a living, what would you like to learn? Would you learn history? Geography? English? Mathematics? Would you learn any of the subjects now taught in school?"*
>
> *"Would you like different subjects? What subjects would you suggest?"*

> *"How do you think your attitude toward school would change?"*
>
> *"Would school be better or worse for you?"*

Using these questions as a start, we might find, as I have on several occasions, that many students don't know why they are asked to learn history. They say that if they didn't need to have their school diploma to earn a living, they would not bother to learn history. The teacher learns that much of what students are asked to do in school makes little sense to them. It is worthwhile to take one subject, history, for example, and use it as a topic of discussion with the following questions:

> *"Have you ever heard of a school where history was not taught?"*
>
> *"Why is history so important that it is taught in every school?"*

If the students don't know why history is taught, you might ask,

> *"Have you ever looked through an old family album and found it interesting to see the pictures of relatives who lived many years ago? Have you ever found that the articles in a museum, especially the articles from many years ago, are really interesting to you? What can we learn from these old albums and old articles? Is what we learn history?"*

If students can't discover from these leading questions some of the reasons why they learn history and why history is interesting and important, I believe the teacher needs to spend some time with her class teaching the relevance of history. Students should be able to do better on these questions than most classes that I have led. In my experience, most of the students haven't the vaguest idea why they study history. Teachers don't discover this until they ask a series of open-ended questions and find that the students can't answer even the most obvious questions relating to history, such as,

> *"Why do we enjoy looking at old family albums and pictures of our relatives from many years back?"*

Even with small children we can develop some of the reasons why students go to school by using the following question:

> *"Suppose your mother said that you should stay home from school today because school is a waste of time. Would you be willing to stay home? If you did stay home, what would you do? Would you watch television? Would you play with your games? Do you think you would enjoy staying home as much as going to school?"*

Putting the unlikely request that the child stay home into the mouth of his own mother piques his interest and often gets a good discussion going.

By using a series of questions exposing the relationship between parents and homework, school discussions can reveal parental attitude about the pressures of school,

> *"Should you do your homework yourself or should your parents help you? What responsibility does your mother have to help you when you are stuck?"*
>
> *"Whom do you go to if your parents don't know how to do a homework assignment that is too hard for you?"*

The meeting is particularly interesting when parents are present and I encourage them to join the discussion later and ask questions of the class.

In districts where there is great parent pressure on students to go to college, higher education is much on the minds of students.

> *"What is the use of going to college?"*
>
> *"Which college would you like to go to?"*
>
> *"Can you get along in life without college?"*
>
> *"Do you know of any great men who succeeded in the world without going to college?"*
>
> *"Is college more important today than it was years ago?"*
>
> *"If it is, do you know why?"*

We can discuss work and the expense of college through the following questions:

> *"How much do you think it costs to go to college?"*
> *"Should students work their way through college?"*
> *"Should students work in high school? In junior high school?"*
> *"Do you believe that you should work in elementary school?"*
> *"How much work should you do?"*
> *"Should boys work more than girls?"*
> *"What kind of work do boys do?"*
> *"What kind of work do girls do?"*
> *"Should you be paid for work you do around your house?"*
> *"Should you donate the work around the house as a contribution to the household?"*
> *"Do you think that work interferes with school work?"*
> *"Do you think that students who work do better or worse in school than those who don't work?"*
> *"Do you think parents should help a child through college?"*
> *"How much help should a parent give?"*
> *"How long should parents help children?"*
> *"How much should parents sacrifice to put a child through college?"*
> *"How much would you want your mother or father to give up? Should they give up a new car, should they give up a new house, should they borrow a lot of money?"*
> *"What obligation does a child have to pay his parents back after he has received the education?"*

Besides school and its relationship to the many subjects mentioned above, there are many social problems suitable for discussion. Probably friendship is the most vital social problem for students in all grades from kindergarten through college. In kindergarten, we should start talking as a whole class about friends and friendship.

> *"How do you make friends?"*
> *"What is a friend?"*
> *"Do you have a friend?"*
> *"What makes a good friend?"*
> *"How do you find a friend?"*
> *"Is it good to have a lot of friends or just a few friends?"*

These questions can be phrased more specifically. As I have said, the more specific a question is, the more it stimulates discussion.

> *"When you first came to school, how did you make a friend?"*
> *"Have you ever moved into a new neighborhood and had no friends at all? How did you find a friend there?"*
> *"What do you do when someone new moves into your neighborhood?"*
> *"Do you wait for him to come to your house or do you go over to his house and try to make friends with him?"*
> *"Do you ever make an effort to help him become friendly with the other children?"*
> *"Have you ever moved to a new neighborhood? If so, how did the other children treat you? How did they treat you, Pete, or you Nick, or you Lanny, when you first came to this school? You were new; how did you make friends?"*

Through a discussion of these questions, some children may learn to make good friends in school. Knowing how to make friends gives one a better chance to succeed in school and in life generally.

Through friendship, one can go on to discuss love. There is controversy over the role the schools should play in family-life education or, as it is popularly called, sex education. Most of the controversy is needless because the main subject to be discussed is not sex but the more important and more inclusive subject of love. Although love can be discussed in any grade in a way that is offensive to no one, it is, for different reasons, almost as taboo as sex. Despite the absence of the immoral connotations that often accompany any discussion of sex, teachers don't know how to talk about love so they shy away from it. This is no particular reflection on teachers because very few people in our society know how to discuss love. It is much more a reflection on our society, in which we almost always unnecessarily associate love with sex. As most of us have never had an opportunity ourselves to discuss the differences, we find ourselves unable to lead a discussion of love divorced from sex. In the lower grades, we might begin with a series of questions such as,

> *"Why do we love?"*
> *"Does anyone love us?"*
> *"Whom do we love?"*
> *"Do we always love our parents?"*
> *"Do we love our brothers and sisters?"*
> *"Do our brothers and sisters love us?"*
> *"Do we love each other in school?"*
> *"Do we love our teacher?"*
> *"Is it important that we love our teacher?"*
> *"Does our teacher love us?"*

Although these questions may seem silly here on paper, they can provide a stimulus for important discussions about love. Children should be made aware of love and aware that it is a subject that they can feel free to talk about. They should also feel free to express their natural warm feelings toward each other and their teachers.

We can vary the questions on love and friendship with another series of questions:

> *"Whom do we want to play with in school?"*
> *"What should we do with a child who doesn't play as well as other children? Should we keep him from the games?"*

Should we help him get into the games even though he can't play very well?"

"Does the class have any explanation for the boy or girl who always wants to have the first turn?"

"What is the best way to explain to him that he must take his turn?"

"What is wrong with the child who is a bully? Does anyone think that he might be lonely?"

"What does the class think about the child who always has to be the center of attention no matter what else is going on in class?"

"What do you think the child gets from all this attention in class?"

"Do you know anyone who is absent a great deal? Can we help him to attend more regularly?"

"Has anyone ever been absent from school when they were not really sick? Why did you stay out of school?"

"Do you think the other children should go to the house of a child who has been absent and try to talk him into coming to school?"

"Is this a responsibility only of the school? Is it our responsibility?"

"If it is our responsibility, why is it?"

"If the absent child doesn't come to school, does it hurt us in any way?"

These are good questions about friendship. They get children thinking about social responsibility.

Children are interested in the subject of conformity. A good way to discuss it is in relationship to the hippies, a group that has wide appeal to most students except the very young.

"Why do people seem to have such a need to conform?"

"Do the hippies, who seem so noncomforming, conform themselves in any way?"

"Why do they grow beards?"

"Why do they wear old clothes?"

"Why do they sometimes say they don't like to bathe?"

"What do they gain from these beliefs and this behavior?"

"Can we examine their beliefs and their behavior and learn something from them?"

"Have there been people like the hippies at other times in the world?"

"Is there anyone in this class who does not conform or who resents having to conform?"

A series of questions on conformity and nonconformity can form the basis for several meetings. Often for the first time children will think about *why* people behave in certain ways.

Meetings are an excellent place to tap a child's imagination. Small children love to use their imaginations; we should be careful not to kill their desire to imagine the unusual by belittling the imagination. As children grow older, we tend to downgrade imagination and elevate solid subjects such as mathematics, history, and social studies. A teacher often feels guilty if she asks children imaginative questions in a regular class. In an open-ended class meeting she need not feel guilty. A teacher can both stimulate thinking and discover much about the children in her class by asking questions such as:

"If you had the power to change into an animal, what animal would you change into?"

"What would you do as this animal?"

"How do you think you would get along with other children and other animals?"

Following these questions in different directions, the teacher will be surprised where the children's imaginations will take them. She should feel free to let the class fantasy as they change into various animals and perhaps even create an animal society within their class.

Children are also vitally interested in monsters.

> *"What kind of a monster would you like to become?"*
> *"What kind of a monster do you like?"*
> *"Are there good monsters?"*
> *"Are all monsters bad?"*
> *"What would you do if you were a monster?"*
> *"If a monster came to live with you, would you like it?"*

Little children never tire of talking about monsters and may even construct a story about monsters. From these and other imagination questions, a teacher can learn how children think, what they worry about, and perhaps discover new ways to relate to her class through understanding more about their imagination.

We can use imaginative questions related to the children's world, such as:

> *"What would you do if tomorrow morning you woke up and you were James Brown? If you were one of the Beatles?"*
> *"Who would you like to be if you could wake tomorrow morning and be someone else?"*
> *"Would you like to be the principal? The teacher?"*
> *"Would you like to be the Superintendent of Schools?"*
> *"Do you have any desire to be the Mayor or the Governor or even the President?"*
> *"If you were the Mayor, what would you do?"*
> *"If you were the Principal, what would you do?"*
> *"How would you treat the children in this class if it were up to you to teach the class?"*
> *"How would you treat the teacher if you were the principal?"*
> *"How would you treat your parents if you were the Mayor or the Governor or the President and your parents were in some kind of difficulty?"*

These last questions place the child in a position where he has to do something. What would he do if he were in a position of power? Sometimes the teacher can let the class act out one of these situations. One child can play a role suggested by one of the previous questions and the other students can take the other necessary parts. The class can then discuss what happened and how the different students played their roles.

Reversal questions are also good to stimulate the children's imagination.

> "If you woke up tomorrow as a girl instead of a boy, how would you behave?"
>
> "If you woke up tomorrow as Negro instead of white, what differences would it make in your life?"
>
> "If you woke up as white instead of Negro, how do you think it would work out?"
>
> "What do you, as the class, think would happen if suddenly all the white people became Negroes or all the Negroes became white? How would it affect you? What do you think you would do? What do you think your parents would do? What would happen in your neighborhood?"

Another kind of question requiring imaginative answers is the following:

> "If your teacher got sick and couldn't come to class, could you get along by yourselves if the principal could not find a substitute? Suppose the class itself had to organize and teach itself for as long as a week, how would you do it? Who would become the leader of the class? Would you need a leader?"
>
> "Do you think you could learn anything without a teacher?"
>
> "How would you spend the day, hour by hour?"

One teacher I know let her class be on their own for a while after such a discussion. They were disorganized and had difficulty functioning by themselves. The teacher held another discussion after the experiment. Having seen the difference between talking about a situation and experiencing it, the children had learned how responsible they would have to be if they had no teacher.

Another good topic is boredom. Children often complain of boredom: school is boring, homework is boring, reading is boring, arithmetic is boring. A class meeting is a good place to examine this complaint and let the children think rather than just complain.

> *"If schools were eliminated completely, how would you spend your time?"*
> *"Would you be bored?"*
> *"What is boredom? How would you explain it?"*
> *"What are some of the times when you have been most bored in your whole life?"*
> *"What are some of the things that most interest you?"*
> *"Are all children bored?"*
> *"Is your mother bored?"*
> *"Is your father bored?"*
> *"Do they complain of boredom?"*
> *"Are some people almost never bored?"*
> *"What is the difference between the people who are bored a lot and those who are not?"*
> *"Is school work always boring?"*
> *"Is there some school work that is never boring?"*
> *"How would you suggest that school work be made less boring?"*

These questions need to be developed slowly. It takes time for children to examine a complaint that they have thought little about. If children can examine what it is that is boring, they may move themselves to use their imagination and their intellect to prevent boredom. They may be able to depend less on others or on television to prevent boredom. We must teach children to develop themselves so that they will not be bored.

Imagination questions can only be stretched so far. Some questions will last for a whole discussion, some for only a short time. To keep a discussion going after the initial questions, the questions must be personal and specific.

Following imagination questions, there are speculation questions. Social studies, for example, is a stimulating subject for speculation.

> *"If the schools ran low on money and two children had to be eliminated from each class, whom would you pick? How could it be done most fairly? Let's see how we would do it right here in this class in a way that would be most fair to everyone."*

Some classes pick two children who are very good because they don't need school. Others pick poor, inattentive students because they are not profiting from school anyway. Some classes elect to make each child stay out for a while so that all can have a chance for education. This question is similar to the Disneyland question in the last chapter. The difference is that it presents a negative rather than a positive situation. The discussion can include what the children could do who would not be allowed to attend school. Could they educate themselves without school?

Some social-studies questions may be used in educational-diagnostic meetings.

> *"Why do we pay taxes?"*
> *"Who pays the most taxes?"*
> *"How should taxes be levied to be most fair?"*

Children are aware of the problems that a child has that may get him involved with the juvenile authorities and with the police. All students should understand what happens to children who get into trouble. Discussing the following questions will give students this understanding.

> *"What should we do with children who are in trouble?"*
> *"Many people say that when you put a boy or girl in juvenile hall it makes them worse. Do you think so?"*
> *"What would you use in place of a juvenile hall or a jail for a child who had committed a serious offense, such as stealing a car?"*

"*We talk a lot about children getting into difficulty, but actually what laws do children break? Let's make up a list and see if we understand all the various kinds of misbehavior that get children into serious trouble?*"

"*Do children and adults agree upon which laws are important?*"

"*Can you think of anything young people do that makes adults very upset but means very little to children? Why is this so?*"

"*Are there differences between laws for adults and laws for children?*"

"*Are our laws fair to children?*"

"*Should children be allowed to smoke in school?*"

"*Should the smoking age be lowered?*"

"*What should we do about children who are caught smoking in school? Who are caught using drugs in school?*"

"*Should children be allowed to drink at age eighteen?*"

"*Should eighteen-year-olds be allowed to vote?*"

"*Should there be special laws for servicemen under twenty-one? For example, should they be allowed to vote? To drink?*"

An entirely new subject is leisure-time activity. We might start with a question about TV.

"*If someone paid you $50 to stop your family from watching television for three days, how would you do it without harming the television set or giving your family some of the money not to watch TV?*"

"*Could you interest them enough in something else so that they would not want to watch television?*"

"*Would you try to do it for $50?*"

"*Would you be willing to forfeit $5 if you failed? In other words, would you bet $5 that you could actually do it provided you could win $50?*"

"For how long could you keep your family from watching TV? Do you think you could do it for one day? Could you do it even for one evening?"

These questions lead to a discussion about our overdependence upon television. Alternatives to television, such as books, could generate a discussion of books and their value. From the initial questions on books, a series of questions leading to new subjects might follow.

"What would you do if there were no books at all?"

"Could school be conducted without books?"

"Would you be satisfied to live without libraries? Without any reading material whatsoever?"

"If you could have only one book, which one would you choose?"

"If you were marooned on a desert island but could somehow have one kind of entertainment, what would you choose?"

"If you were marooned on an uninhabited island, could you figure out a way to get off?"

"What might you use to help you?"

"What would you look for on the island that might help you to escape?"

"If you crashed in an airplane, could you salvage parts of the airplane that would help you?"

"What have you learned in school that might help you to get off the island?"

"Have you learned anything in school that would help you survive if you were lost anywhere else?"

"Suppose you were lost in the desert?"

"Suppose you were lost in the mountains?"

"How would you get along in a strange city where they spoke a language that you did not know?"

"What would you try to tell the people? How would you approach them?"

Many of these questions relate to science as well as to social studies. In fact, an entire science curriculum could be based on questions about survival. The seemingly easy but really difficult problem of lighting a fire without matches could be discussed and then turned into a class project. Could the class do what they had talked about? I doubt that many fifth or sixth graders could start a fire without a match. We take the ease of flint and steel too much for granted. A discussion might follow about how much we take what we have for granted.

Because current urban conditions are covered in newspapers and magazines, questions such as the following might stimulate students to read.

> *"What would you do if the smog got so bad that cars could no longer be used?"*
>
> *"Would you drive your car if you knew that a certain number of people were dying from smog?"*
>
> *"Suppose we had no cars or buses in Los Angeles. How would people get around?"*
>
> *"Can you suggest ways to solve the smog problem?"*
>
> *"How important are cars? Are they used much more than they need to be?"*
>
> *"Suppose your father and mother could no longer drive. How would you get around the city?"*

Many questions about family life, especially divorce and marriage, can be effective with older children.

> *"Do you think that people should be allowed to get divorced?"*
>
> *"What is the effect upon children when parents get divorced?"*
>
> *"Does it bother older children more or younger children more?"*

The discussion can become very personal and thus, usually, very important. In one class meeting, for example, the teacher asked, "What important decisions do you have to make?" A little boy raised his hand and said, "My parents are getting divorced and I have to decide whether I will live with my mother or my father." The discussion that followed helped prepare all the children to be able to handle social problems that might arise in their lives.

Marriage and readiness for marriage should be covered in depth in high schools.

> "How long should you know someone before you get married?"
>
> "How much time should there be between engagement and marriage?"
>
> "Should divorce be made easier?"
>
> "How old should you be before you get married?"
>
> "Should you have to stay married for a certain time before you could get divorced?"
>
> "Should parents be allowed to get divorced?"

Junior high and older elementary students can also have good discussions based on these questions. More questions on family life are:

> "Do you want to have children?"
>
> "How many children do you want?"
>
> "How would you raise your children?"
>
> "How would you be different from your parents?"
>
> "How many of you don't want to have children?"
>
> "If you don't want children, why? Let's have a discussion between those who want children and those who don't."
>
> "What good are children anyway?"
>
> "How do children help adults?"
>
> "How do adults help children?"

In talking about children, students learn much about themselves, their relationship with each other, and their relationship with their parents. Teachers can also learn how children relate to adults and to each other. This understanding will help a

sensitive teacher in dealing with social problems that may arise
in her class.

Family-life discussions can also be related to school subjects
such as mathematics. One reason that children have difficulty
with mathematics is that we do not relate it to their lives. Many
discussions can easily be tied to the ideas of mathematics. We
might ask young children the following:

> *"Suppose your father didn't have time to buy your mother
> a birthday present and gave you $5 to buy the present.
> What would you buy her?"*
>
> *"Where would you spend the money?"*
>
> *"Would you add some money of your own for the
> present?"*
>
> *"If your father couldn't give you any money, how would
> you earn money to buy a present for your mother?"*
>
> *"If you earned money, would you give some of it to your
> family?"*
>
> *"Would you help your father support the family if you
> knew that he needed the help?"*
>
> *"Under what circumstances would you not give your fam-
> ily any money?"*
>
> *"How much does it cost, for instance, to make a birthday
> party?"*
>
> *"How much does it cost to keep a child?"*
>
> *"How much money does it take for a whole family to be
> comfortable?"*
>
> *"Do grownups worry a great deal about money?"*
>
> *"If they do, why?"*
>
> *"How important is money? Can people be happy without
> it?"*

Money is a stimulating topic; almost every mathematical discussion I have with young children is concerned with money. It is
difficult to talk abstractly about numbers with elementary
school students.

Another subject of interest to children is health. Although we talk a lot about health, we rarely find out what children understand about it. For example:

> *"What happens to you when you are sick?"*
> *"What does it feel like when you have the flu?"*
> *"What happens to you when you have the chicken pox?"*
> *"How do people who have poor eyesight get along?"*
> *"How do people who have poor hearing get along?"*
> *"How do you think you'd get along if you couldn't see?"*
> *"What is being blind?"*
> *"What is being deaf?"*
> *"Can one live a normal life if he is blind?"*
> *"Can a deaf person learn to speak?"*
> *"What do doctors do?"*
> *"What do hospitals do?"*
> *"What do nurses do?"*

This series of questions about sickness, doctors, and hospitals can produce a good exchange of ideas.

It is not the purpose of this chapter to provide an exact recipe for classroom meetings. Rather it is to help teachers appreciate the almost unlimited material suitable for group discussion. Anything of interest to anyone in the class is a possible subject for discussion at any age. Children will discuss ideas readily once they believe that the discussion is worthwhile, that others are listening to them, and that everyone gets an opportunity to participate. They are anxious to relate to the world, to discover that school is interested in the world, and to learn that the world can be brought into the school. By allowing the children to discover that what they and the others in the class have to say is valuable and important, the discussions raise their self-esteem and promote involvement. They are almost always relevant and thought-provoking. Done well, these discussions are fun, and learning that is fun is scarce.

CHAPTER THIRTEEN

Morality

Morality is an emotional subject that causes so much controversy that schools do not ordinarily teach or even discuss it. I believe that certain moral values can be taught in school if the teaching is restricted to principles about which there is essentially no disagreement in our society. Generally accepted moral principles that lend themselves to discussion in the schools are that it is better for both us and our children to live without lying, cheating, blackmailing, and stealing. We have an obligation to our children to provide, both at home and at school, an environment in which they can both learn about and behave according to these principles. To the extent that we fail to provide such an environment in our homes and at school, we fail our children.

We often try to teach morality by preaching commandment-like strictures coupled with "You'd better do it or you'll be punished." This procedure is rarely effective. Here I shall suggest what I believe can be an effective alternative to preaching and threats. By using the class as a social-problem-solving group, moral behavior can be presented as a part of life rather than as dogma. The goal is to implement moral behavior through honest discussion aimed at matching our actions to our words.

A class meeting that demonstrated both the need for and the

possibility of teaching morality in school occurred with a sixth-grade class in a school in the harbor area of Los Angeles. The audience of about 250 people consisted of the thirty principals in my class, the school faculty, teachers from nearby schools, some local school board members, and about half the children's parents. Starting with a common school problem, but ultimately centering on the larger problem of lying, the discussion both startled and enlightened the audience. The children, who seemed exceptionally bright and alert, complained that the principal had stopped free play on the playground because there was too much arguing, shouting, and fighting. After he assigned specific play areas to the sixth graders, most of the problems stopped. The sixth graders complained that the principal treated them as infants and that the group was being punished for the transgressions of a few; they said that they wanted their old playground privileges to be restored. I asked the class whether, during the meeting, they could work out a plan to present to the principal for getting privileges back. The principal, who was present, said he was willing to accept any reasonable plan, but so far the class hadn't presented one to him. One reason for the class's lack of constructive suggestions was that, until this meeting, they had never had a chance to meet together to discuss the problem. (Next year the teacher plans to hold class meetings regularly.)

Not used to solving problems, the class, in the first part of the meeting, both complained that they were being unfairly restricted and promised that they wouldn't break the rules anymore if they had another chance. It was hard for them to think about formulating a plan for better order on the playground. Not understanding that they were expected to think and plan, they preferred to wheedle and promise. Although they offered many suggestions that required the principal to change his behavior, they steadfastly refused to examine their own behavior or to take any responsibility for their loss of privileges. Finally, after much discussion in which I had to point out over and over that they were begging or excusing rather than planning, they proposed that they all sign a petition asking for their privileges back and saying that they all would obey the rules of the playground. The class seemed satisfied with the plan. To test their commitment to it, I asked what they would do if someone who signed the petition broke a rule.

The class thought my question presented an insurmountable problem because, according to almost everyone, the child who broke the rule would never admit it. I asked, "Do you mean that, even after he signed the petition saying he would obey the rules, he would lie and get the whole class in trouble rather than admit that he broke a rule?" The class agreed that he would lie, that any of them would lie, because they were afraid of punishment. I said, "Would you rather have the whole class punished than tell the truth, spare the class, and take the consequences of your actions yourself?" After much discussion, the students concluded that it is easier to lie; they were so used to lying that telling the truth in a situation such as this would be very unusual indeed. In fact, they said it would be so unusual that they "just plain wouldn't do it." Therefore, the petition and the signatures and the promises and the plan would all go down the drain because, under pressure, no one would tell the truth to preserve the privileges of the class.

I then told the class that it seemed to me they had a more fundamental problem than losing playground privileges. The fundamental problem concerned truth: specifically, should they tell the truth? The students unanimously agreed that telling the truth was right, moral, just, and good. In actual practice, however, they preferred to lie. One girl went so far as to say in all sincerity (I still can remember the conviction written on her face when she said it), "Dr. Glasser, if I told the truth, my whole world would collapse." Interestingly enough, although they had little confidence in the adult world to provide moral leadership, they did say that they had great confidence in their teacher: "She never lies to us."

I am not implying, nor do I believe, that schools teach children to lie. Nevertheless, it seems to me that the schools should be concerned that they have created an environment in which the children agree that, under stress or the threat of punishment, they would almost always lie, even at the expense of the rest of their own class. To answer the argument that problems of morality belong strictly to the home or church, I can say only that I believe that, whatever the effectiveness of the home and church, when a problem of morality exists in school, the school should not avoid it. By no stretch of the imagination can these children be considered different from the popular impression of the average American child. They are the Dicks and Janes of the primers in reading, with the opportunities, advantages, and lack of socioeconomic problems associated with the wonderful, bright children that populate the textbooks of America. Nevertheless, they are liars and, as the discussion continued, they said that they are also experts in cheating, stealing, and blackmail. They assume that lying, cheating, stealing, and blackmail are a natural part of life in the real world and that the world demands this kind of behavior from the individual if he is to survive. Maybe the children are right, but I do not think so. I am unwilling to accept a totally immoral world, and I believe that children need not accept an immoral world either. Whatever the world is like, each individual still has a choice about his own behavior.

Asked for their opinion on whether or not adults lied, the children agreed that adults lied often and that they stole and cheated as well. They would have talked in some detail about their experiences with their own parents, but because of the large audience, I felt discretion was in order. I cut off this tack by saying, "Let's stick to the problem of the class." This is a good suggestion for a leader to make whenever he is in doubt about the propriety of a discussion. A balance must be struck between complete honesty and what the community will bear. The children did talk about the lying, cheating, and stealing that their brothers and sisters did. Blackmail in the home was common. A child who discovered a brother or sister doing something wrong would extract work, favors, or money under the threat of exposure to their parents. All of the children were stoic about being caught and punished often. They looked at punishment as the luck of the game. It didn't stop them from lying; it merely encouraged them to become more crafty. Furthermore, punishment, when it did occur, was the price they paid for their lies. Once the price was paid, they were free to lie again; hopefully, they would not be caught the next time.

Everyone in the audience was uncomfortably aware that the children were expressing their keen evaluation of the world. Elementary school pupils understand early in life that we really live in two worlds, the world of pretense, where we spout the moral values, and the world of reality, where we pay as little attention to them as possible. The audience, well knowing both of these worlds, had never been made so acutely aware that the children also knew how phony the world is. Perhaps partly to avoid admitting to themselves that their own actions were often inconsistent with their professed beliefs, the adults were shocked at the awareness of the children. As part of their world of pretense, the adults thought that the children should not have learned about the real world so soon. In the audience discussion that followed the class meeting, as the adults came more to accept the children's knowledge of the real world, most of the audience agreed that the schools should begin to teach children ways to live in which they had less need to lie. Although I said that I thought class meetings could play a major role in teaching morality in the schools, it was clear at the end of this one meeting that getting the children to stop lying would be difficult.

Living in a world in which they are inconsistently caught but consistently punished when they are caught, the children said again and again that when they did something wrong and were caught, they were rarely given an opportunity to try to solve the

problem. Few parents, catching a child in a misdeed, stop to
discuss in a warm, meaningful way how the child might have
behaved differently. Almost always the child is told flatly that
he is wrong, punished, and admonished not to do it again. The
children were also clear in their belief that, as long as we rely
upon punishment, we will sow the seeds of lying, cheating,
stealing, and blackmail.

problem. Few parents, catching a child in a misdeed, stop to discuss in a warm, meaningful way how the child might have behaved differently. Almost always the child is told flatly that he is wrong, punished, and admonished not to do it again. The children were also clear in their belief that, as long as we rely upon punishment, we will sow the seeds of lying, cheating, stealing, and blackmail.

When I asked the children if they could stop lying if no punishment followed their telling the truth, they said that it would take a long time to develop enough trust in anyone to change their pattern. They thought that eventually they might learn to tell the truth. Finally I asked them if they would commit themselves to the truth—no lying—from nine o'clock that night, when the meeting finished, until two o'clock the following afternoon, when the teacher would hold another meeting. Could they rely on truth alone for seventeen hours? After thinking it over, they said, almost unanimously, that it would not be possible. They tried to get me to understand just how difficult it is to rely on the truth, and that they couldn't possibly do so for anywhere near seventeen hours. They said they would like to rely on truth but they had not found ways to do so. I then modified my request by asking them to discuss, in the next day's class meeting, the situations in which they felt they had to lie, and to look for possible truthful alternatives. Such a discussion would at least get things started, and they agreed.

Two bright results did come from the meeting. First, the students wanted to learn to live so that they would not need to lie all the time. Unhappy and dissatisfied with lying, they could see no way to escape punishment when they told the truth. Second, the students were convinced that their teachers never lied to them. Had they believed that their teachers lied to them, I doubt that we could ever get them to stop lying. Considering what the children said, however, I think lying can be reduced by holding class meetings and by eliminating punishment.

Everyone that evening was moved by what he had seen. We were disturbed by an adult world that had caused these young children to have so little faith that following our professed moral values would lead to a satisfactory life. Most of the audience agreed that morality should be discussed in the schools and that class meetings combined with no punishment might be effective in helping the children toward better behavior. Although the children had doubts natural to anything new, they were willing to make the attempt. They would not have been so open and so honest had they not wished to change. I am afraid this openness and honesty will soon disappear. As I discussed with the audience, were I to address similar questions to the teachers, administrators, and community leaders present, the honest, open participation demonstrated by the sixth graders would be unlikely.

I believe that morality should be discussed in the schools. The discussions should be part of a nonthreatening, nonpunitive environment. It is important that children commit themselves to the truth; it is just as important that they examine in detail in the class meetings the problems in their lives that cause them to lie, and that they try to solve these problems and learn the value of the truth. If they cannot personally experience the value of truth, truth will have no meaning to them. It is not enough, therefore, to hold social-problem-solving meetings. We must create both at home and at school a nonpunitive, open, honest, problem-solving environment in which children can live a moral life, not just pay lip service to it. In schools without such an environment, morality and responsibility will be only words for most children.

CHAPTER FOURTEEN

Discipline and School Administration

A school cannot function without an effective administration that develops reasonable rules and enforces them. Students should have a voice in making the rules that apply to them; once rules are established, however, students are expected to follow them. A recent experience with an Upward Bound program at UCLA can be used as an example of potentially excellent education foundering because of serious misunderstandings over what responsibility should be taken by students and what responsibility must be accepted by educational administrators.

A part of the national antipoverty program, Upward Bound seeks first to identify intellectually capable children who, because of their environment, poverty, or poor schooling, have not been able to realize their potential, and then to prepare them for higher education by an intensive educational experience on a college campus. It is believed, and wisely so, that if these children had a successful and stimulating school experience, they would likely be motivated to go to college and become leaders in their communities. By their example, they would stimulate others. The phrase Upward Bound illustrates the concept: to elevate a community through the use of its inherent intellectual resources.

In previous chapters, I have described how memory-fact education and lack of relevance fail to give children the emotional satisfaction and motivation to continue in school. The consequent dropouts are most common in the central city; it is there also that behavior problems are most acute. Most educators recognize that we need better ways than we have now to help students toward better behavior in school. The class meetings are an attempt to meet this need. At present, in both elementary and secondary schools, we usually establish rigid rules that lead to punishment when they are broken. The rigid rules of the average central-city school cause even those who have most to gain, the intelligent, to rebel and to refuse to accept the education available. Because an inflexible, punitive approach works poorly, well-meaning, sociologically trained experts—including those who establish the educational philosophy for federal programs such as Upward Bound—have insisted that central-city children, most of whom have difficulty obeying rules, need a permissive environment with few rules and little enforcement. They wrongly equate deprivation with a special need to do immediately as one wishes, not understanding that the children have not yet learned to behave in a permissive environment in ways that will be beneficial to them.

Reasonable rules, firmly enforced through separation from the program (not punishment) and backed up by problem-solving class meetings, are a necessary part of helping students become responsible enough to take advantage of what is made available to them. Those who would completely relax rules are so anxious to please "deprived" children that they fail to understand that firm, fair standards of discipline mean that we care; lax standards are interpreted by those who need firm standards as lack of interest. This view is confirmed by the results of a twelve-year study in self-esteem carried out by Dr. Stanley Coopersmith. The following is quoted from an article by Dr. Coopersmith in the February, 1968, *Scientific American:*

A second and more surprising finding was that the parents of the high-self-esteem children proved to be less permissive than those of children with lower self-esteem. . . . They demanded high standards of behavior and were strict and consistent in enforcement of the rules. Yet their discipline was by no means harsh; indeed, these parents were less punitive than the parents of the boys whom we found to be lacking in self-esteem. They used rewards rather than corporal punishment or withdrawal of love as disciplinary techniques, and their sons praised their fairness. We found that the parents of the low-self-esteem boys, on the other hand, tended to be extremely permissive but inflicted harsh punishment when the children gave them trouble. These boys considered their parents unfair, and they took the absence of definitely stated rules and limits for their behavior as a sign of lack of parental interest in them.

The family life of the high-self-esteem boys was marked not only by the existence of a well-defined constitution for behavior but also by a democratic spirit. The parents established the principles and defined the powers, privileges and responsibilities of the members, but they presided as benevolent despots: they were respectful toward dissent, open to persuasion and generally willing to allow the children a voice in the making of family plans. It seems safe to conclude that all these factors—deep interest in the children, the guidance provided by well-defined rules of expected behavior, nonpunitive treatment and respect for the children's views—contributed greatly to the development of the boys' high self-esteem.*

In contrast to the parents of the high-self-esteem boys, traditional education often produces problems that stem from poorly conceived and poorly administered rules. The following experience clearly shows these problems.

An Upward Bound program was conducted at UCLA during 1967. There are about nine weeks of full-time, live-in school during the summer. Afterwards, during the regular high school

* From "Studies in Self-Esteem," by Dr. Stanley Coopersmith. Copyright © February, 1968, by Scientific American, Inc. All rights reserved.

year, the group meets at UCLA each Saturday for four hours. Students who started as sophomores could participate for three years. I was asked to consult when the summer program was more than half over. When I am asked to present my ideas, I am usually given a free hand. In this case, I suggested to the assistant director that she assemble both students and staff so that I could talk to them together. Wanting to find out from both groups where they thought the program was in difficulty, I had nothing to say to the staff that the students should not hear. The assistant director thought the program was in serious trouble and hoped that I might be able to help. My experience that followed with the Upward Bound students, most of whom had been recruited from the central-city high schools of Los Angeles, was both enlightening and upsetting.

First of all, the attendance at the initial meeting was sparse. Of the 105 students, perhaps twenty attended; of about thirty faculty, perhaps eight attended. It was not just that most of the students and faculty apparently had little interest in what any outside "expert" had to say. I found an atmosphere of discouragement and failure that led to lackadaisical attendance at all scheduled activities. After another meeting a week later and after more detailed discussion with the staff, I saw that the assistant director was correct in her appraisal: the program was indeed in serious trouble. Given the objective of preparing students for higher education, there were, in my opinion, some major flaws in the way the program was being carried out. In the initial discussion, the students showed a remarkable lack of interest in the educational objectives of the program. They thought that the program was primarily an experience in social living. They believed that they would benefit from the program by learning to live together in a mixed racial group, by having a close association with their teachers and counselors, and by getting the feel of living on a university campus.

Much less positive about the academic part of the program, the students stated clearly at both meetings that they didn't consider binding the commitment they had initially made to attend class. The students who regularly attended class (probably less than 30 out of the total of 105) were considered "square." Many students attempted to impress me with the importance of the social milieu. They also said that the classes were dull, the instructors boring, and the discussions repetitive; in any case, formal education wasn't really the main problem. The students' attitude, which could be described as "everything will be all right as long as we are happy and well-adjusted," struck me as a distortion of progressive education into no education at all. I would have been less concerned were it not apparent that the students had here an opportunity for an excellent educational experience. They were throwing away what for many would be their last chance for education.

The program directors told me that they could not enforce class attendance or any other rules because their superiors believed that subjecting the students to disciplinary action would cause the program to fail. As far as I could see, the students regarded the program as a lark. It was a chance to get out of their ordinary surroundings and enjoy themselves while getting paid $10 a week. In addition, it was an opportunity to vent their pent-up educational frustration against their dedicated but in many cases totally untrained instructors—untrained, that is, in dealing with the students they were now asked to teach.

The educational format of the program was excellent. The classes were small (about twelve to a class), the teachers tried to make the education relevant, the teachers were always accessible to the students, and special tutors were hired to work with individual students who were deficient in basic subject material. No grades were given, and the program had few of the educational mediocrities described in Chapter 6. Yet, instead of the excellent motivation that I believe is possible through the use of these educational techniques, there was chaos. I could not understand how the teachers stood it through the summer;

when I talked to them, they were apathetic and discouraged. After five weeks of the program, little remained of whatever educational enthusiasm they may have had initially.

What went wrong? Potentially good education was going to waste. The students didn't even come to class. Teachers complained that class attendance was so erratic that continuity was impossible. Six would show up one day, three the next; only a few came every day. Sometimes no one showed up. One of the teachers was afraid to dismiss her class for a break because no one returned afterwards. The Upward Bound program had achieved exactly one-half of what a good educational program should achieve; the teachers were motivated and to the best of their ability provided a good educational environment; the students, on the other hand, had made no commitment at all.

After meeting with the students and the faculty, I attempted to analyze where the breakdown had occurred and why the students had made no commitment. I know from experience that it is possible for students such as these from poor backgrounds to respond with dedication to good educational opportunities. A major part of the problem was the destructive atmosphere that prevailed. The faculty and the administrators believed that these were poor, deprived, miserable students who had never really had a chance for education. They also believed that the condition of the students was the fault of the social system and the schools. Although the regular schools that the students attend are not the best in the community, neither are they so bad as necessarily to produce students in the preconceived image of the staff. Similarly, although the students do not live comfortably according to the standards of many readers of this book, most of the students considered their living conditions to be tolerable. And lastly, although prejudice against Negroes and Mexican Americans certainly exists, the students in honest discussion could not state that they themselves had experienced the degree of prejudice that was considered, in the atmosphere of the Upward Bound program, to be such a handicap to them.

For the program to succeed, therefore, the staff would have to start by following one principle of Reality Therapy: *All students must be accepted as potentially capable, not as handicapped by their environment.* We cannot change their past or their present surroundings, but we can give them the opportunity for a good education. Unless they take advantage of this opportunity and themselves overcome whatever obstacles confront them, they will fail in life. It is harmful to expect little of "have-nots" because they have not. When this happened to the students in Upward Bound, they responded with self-destructive behavior, confirming their long-standing inability to recognize a good opportunity. We can't help people by feeling sorry for them; they neither need nor want our sympathy. The students might have survived this "welfare" atmosphere had it not led first to administrative indecision and finally to abdication of the responsibility to enforce the reasonable rules. The excuse for failing to enforce the rules was the old saw previously stated: The children had been subjected to too many rules; they were angry, frustrated, and problem-bound; and any attempt to force them to conform to reasonable standards of behavior would be harmful to them.

In the beginning of the program, the students had been told that attendance in class and in the tutoring sessions was mandatory. When they failed to come to class and failed to attend the tutoring sessions, however, no systematic effort was made to deal with the problem. Based on my ten years of work at the Ventura School with girls from backgrounds similar to those of the students, I believe that they could interpret the failure to enforce the rules only as a demonstration that the staff did not care about them. If education is as important as the program and staff profess, if it is the best chance these students have to escape failure in life, the staff must get the students to attend class to make up their academic deficiencies and to move ahead. The teachers confirmed that they were behind in almost every subject. The students, reacting to the staff as if the staff were not interested (which was their interpretation of the staff's failure to enforce class attendance), attended class even less and became less interested in education.

The students will be harmed further by their failure to attend class when they return to public school. Class attendance is not optional in the public schools. In meetings that I held with the students, they emphasized that they attended class in public school. Although they were not necessarily doing well, they had not dropped out. Unfortunately, in Upward Bound they learned that class attendance isn't important.

As I stated in the beginning of the chapter, school children should have some part in making the rules of their school. They do not decide, however, whether or not rules, once established, should be enforced. They may choose to disobey the rules; this choice is open to all. But they then have to accept the consequences of their choice. Offering good education in a stimulating setting, Upward Bound has even more rationale than the average public school to enforce the rules. Students might argue that the memorizing education of the public school does not stimulate class attendance, but that reasoning is not applicable to Upward Bound.

Many colleges do not have attendance rules. College administrators have found that they are not necessary because college students have learned to behave more responsibly than their high school and junior high school fellows. This example, however, shows only that it is reasonable to relax rules as people become responsible. Whenever students of any age show sufficient maturity to benefit, without rules, from the education that is offered them, I am in favor of doing away with rules.

For most students who have not done well in school, permissiveness is destructive. Ultimately it generates antagonism and ridicule toward those who unrealistically administer without rules. None of the educational suggestions made in this book imply that students should be given responsibilities that they are not ready or willing to assume. Part of the benefit of the social-problem-solving class meeting is that it teaches the students that they have a responsibility toward their teachers. If a teacher attends class, the student also has a responsibility to attend class unless he is excused by the teacher.

Responsibility is not a one-way street. Reasonable rules are part of a thoughtful, problem-solving education. Educational effectiveness cannot be increased by irregular class attendance. Teachers have the responsibility to make education relevant and interesting; students have the responsibility to *attend class, to study, and to learn.*

All rules should be examined carefully. Rules considered necessary should be enforced; the others should be dropped. If, for example, the Upward Bound program directors believe that class attendance should be optional, the rules should say so. If they believe, and if the rules state, that class attendance is mandatory, the rule should be enforced. Optional class attendance cannot lead to success for these academically lagging students. I would suggest, therefore, that all students selected for Upward Bound be asked to sign an agreement stating they will attend classes and tutoring sessions. If they miss a determined number of classes (I suggest five), they should be removed from the program. Problem-solving groups should be a part of the program. One use of the groups should be to discuss and try to help students who miss even one class. Each student should have the responsibility to help every other student attend class. When I suggested in a group meeting with the Upward Bound students that each student had an obligation to every other student, they bitterly attacked the word "obligation." They had no experience in social responsibility, no experience in problem solving, and little feeling of concern for one another when the concern meant more than just talking— when it meant getting involved in helping a student to go to class. They could not develop a sense of obligation in an environment of optional class attendance.

It will be argued that a student dismissed from the program will go down the drain into certain educational failure. My experience at the Ventura School, however, shows just the opposite. Given the choice between dismissal and a good educational program, given the feeling that teachers and administrators care about education and students (and demonstrate their concern by getting students to class), a student will come to class and will appreciate the concern that has gotten him there. Anyone who leaves the program because, to quote one, "That's conformity, man, and I don't dig it," will soon find himself leading a far more conforming life of failure. He should be given the chance to reevaluate his decision not to attend. Each time a student is dropped, it should be for a definite and perhaps slowly increasing time, but always with the option to come back and try again. For example, a student who doesn't attend class in the beginning could be dropped for three days. Then, if he comes back and still doesn't attend, he could be dropped for a week. A third failure to attend would bring a suspension for most of the remainder of the summer session. Returning and attending class after any suspension would make a student eligible to continue in the program on Saturdays all year and to return the following year. If he did not attend class even after the suspensions, he would still be eligible to try again the following summer, but he would not be able to attend the Saturday sessions during the year. The student should not be punished. He should merely be told that he is being given an opportunity to make a choice. The choice, however, is not whether or not he wants to obey the rules; it is between participating fully in the program or leaving it to see what he can do on his own.

Partly because I came into the program after it was more than half over and partly because the program directors were not at first receptive to my suggestions, they were not adopted at the time. I was told that they might be used the following year. These suggestions will, I believe, give the program a chance for success that it does not now have.

The situation that occurred in the Upward Bound program cannot occur in regular high school because attendance is mandatory there; the student either goes to school or drops out. If all the suggestions made in this book for solving problems in public school do not work for any individual student, the only discipline that makes sense is exclusion with the opportunity to return and try again, exactly as suggested for the Upward Bound program. Better education as described in Chapters 1 through 8 will help students stay in school; the problem-solving techniques described in Chapters 9 through 12 will help to motivate them to continue their education. Separate from the philosophy and the recommendations of this book, these administrative suggestions will be less effective. If my suggestions for discipline are taken totally out of context and represented as "Follow our rules or be kicked out," they make no sense. Rules should be reasonable; they should be changed when conditions change; they should, when possible, be decided upon jointly by faculty and students; and they should be enforced.

CHAPTER FIFTEEN

The Pershing School

In the fall of 1962, I had the opportunity to address the administrators of the Sacramento area public schools. At this time, the ideas of Reality Therapy were poorly formed, the relationship between these ideas and the public schools still in its infancy. Important then, and still the basis of Reality Therapy, was the concept of involvement. To change toward more successful behavior, one must become involved with a responsible person, who may be a therapist or teacher. Because the audience consisted of school personnel, the importance of teacher-pupil involvement was emphasized; lack of involvement was shown to be a major cause of behavior disturbances and educational failures in school. Although much of my presentation was oriented toward the correctional school at Ventura, Mr. Donald O'Donnell, principal of the Pershing Elementary School (a 600-student school in the San Juan School District, near Sacramento) spoke to me of his own belief that the key to educational success was creating an environment of warm, personal involvement among the students and teachers. From then until now, I have worked in the Pershing School as a consultant and, more important to me, as a student of what I believe is one of the most innovative and important elementary school programs in the country.

Inspired by the imagination and guidance of Mr. O'Donnell, a school program has been developed that involves teachers and pupils in an unusually wide variety of intensive educational experiences. The Pershing School has excellent teachers, but there is nothing that these teachers do that could not be duplicated in most public schools. The financing is ordinary. The pupils come from a middle-class neighborhood of Sacramento where education is important but where it doesn't receive the disproportionate emphasis that it does in our more wealthy suburbs. The Pershing School has an extra teacher paid with funds available to any school that has "educationally handicapped" children, that is, children with serious educational problems. A second extra teacher is paid through a state program for remedial reading. The funds for both of these special programs need not necessarily be used for salaries; they may be used for any *bona fide* educational purpose, such as books or supplies. The programs described in this chapter utilize the extra teachers in several ways, but even before they were available, the programs were in limited operation through the active participation of the principal in the daily teaching program.

To quote Mr. O'Donnell:

Attempts have been made to solve educational problems through increased appropriations of money and through the use of this money to buy better books, visual aids, and other materials. By itself, this approach has been generally unsuccessful. At Pershing, we used the little extra money to add people, not supplies, to give as many students as possible involvement with responsible people. With these additional people, our program has grown.

Mr. O'Donnell goes on to point out that the money he has obtained for the additional teachers at Pershing is available to any California school and to schools in many other states.

After I first became aware of the program at Pershing, I described it to my family. My daughter, then in elementary school, thought for a minute and said, "Dad, you are always

saying that you don't like a stripped-down car. Compared to
Pershing, I go to a stripped-down school." Although some
people call the extra programs at the Pershing School "educational frills," Mr. O'Donnell does not believe that it is a frill to
have children involved with many good teachers, to give them
individual and small-group attention, to extend the educational
program far beyond the limitations of the regular curriculum,
and to give children an opportunity to create without being
judged or graded. On the last point, Mr. O'Donnell defines
creativity carefully. He does not expect children to create great
works of art, literature, or music. To him, the creative child is a
child who discovers something important on his own. Whether
or not his discovery has been discovered before is unimportant
to O'Donnell. The creative process is the discovery of something new to the child. He gets the same thrill as the original
discoverer, a thrill that motivates him to keep searching, to keep
discovering.

At the Pershing School the children are heterogeneously
grouped; that is, all students, including the gifted, the retarded,
and the disturbed, are placed together in classes at their age
level. Special needs and problems are dealt with through a series
of programs that reach both into the classroom and out from the
classroom according to the needs of the heterogeneous group.
Mr. O'Donnell uses heterogeneous grouping because it is similar to the community and the world. Students can learn what
they have to offer to the group and what they can receive from
the group.

Most schools, including the Pershing School, are concerned
with the young child who has difficulty in following the school
rules and in learning. As described above, the state provides
extra funds for these educationally handicapped students. The
Pershing School was thus able to free one of its teachers, Keith
Maxwell, to direct the program for the educationally handicapped in the first three grades. It is in the first three grades that
these students' problems must be solved. Special programs past

third grade have little effect on the child who has had difficulty since entering school. Experience at Pershing shows that, using the special programs, most of these children can solve their problems before the fourth grade. In contrast to most programs in which the extra teacher removes these students from the classroom and teaches them in a special class of their own, the Pershing School keeps them in their own class. Mr. Maxwell has worked out a detailed program to help them without removing them and thus giving them the failure identity that accompanies them when they are put into a separate, special class. To keep the students he was trying to help in the regular class, Mr. Maxwell has had to subordinate his role to that of the classroom teacher; she is in charge, and she directs his participation in her class. Available each morning to assist four primary teachers (the number he believes he can serve adequately), he tells the teachers that he is ready to help them. They can use his services as they see fit; he will help them with any child in the class in any way that he can. Although he has been funded to deal exclusively with the educationally handicapped, and his program has been most effective for them, he is available to work with any child. Thus the likelihood is reduced that a child who works with him either in or out of class will be labeled a failure either by himself or by others.

Some teachers, at least in the beginning, adopted the attitude, "Stay out." They felt that they were capable of handling their own students and that they did not need his help. He did not go into their rooms and imply, "I am an expert. I will help you with the children who have so many problems. I can do it better than you." He made himself available and he waited until he was asked. Because he had been a teacher in the school and because the classroom teachers recognized that there were many problems, he was soon asked.

When the teachers first asked for help, they said the traditional, "Take them out." They wanted Mr. Maxwell to take the disturbed children out of the class, work with them separately, fix them up, and then return them to the class. Although neither Mr. O'Donnell, Mr. Maxwell, nor I believe in this educational philosophy, it had to be followed because of the teacher's request. Meanwhile, in conferences with the teachers, Mr. Maxwell explained what else he was willing and able to do and told of his doubts about the "take them out" philosophy. He discovered, as have many other teachers, that he could take students out of class and teach them, yet when they returned to their class they could not repeat what they had done individually or in the small group with Mr. Maxwell. A child who read well in a separate room with Mr. Maxwell often could not read for his classroom teacher.

After Mr. Maxwell told the teachers that he thought he could work effectively right in the classroom, some of the teachers said, "Come in; work with the small group of disturbed children in the corner while I continue with the rest of the class so we can move ahead." The teacher understands the children and their problems better when she observes someone else struggling with them. Because the two teachers are together, communication is free and open; there is opportunity for an immediate discussion about any child. As the class teachers observed Mr. Maxwell working with the small group in the corner, they wanted to try it themselves. The next step then was, "Come in, you take my class, and I will work with the small group." Again, the class teacher set the pace. Mr. Maxwell took the class and the teacher worked with the small group, still in the classroom. Children in both the large and small groups benefited from the combined efforts of their teacher and Mr. Maxwell.

In the last two examples in which either Mr. Maxwell or the class teacher worked with the small group, the group may have been disturbed children, gifted children, a mixture of both, or any other grouping the classroom teacher designated. As the helping teacher, Mr. Maxwell must be receptive to work in any way the classroom teacher suggests. If he has a different opinion, he discusses it with her, but she decides when, where, and how he implements his suggestions.

In another variation, the classroom teacher said, "Come in; I want to take a small group out." While Mr. Maxwell taught the class, she took the small group outside of the classroom and did something with them that made sense to her. Again she was in charge and she figured out what she wanted to do. The children had another new and to them exciting experience under new conditions with their teacher.

A final approach, one I believe unique to the Pershing School in the use of the extra teacher, occurred when the classroom teacher said, "Go to another room, take that teacher's class, and send her here to help me." Any teacher in the school who wished to participate became available as a special teacher to help the classroom teacher in any way the classroom teacher requested. Under these circumstances, many children got to know, in various situations, their own teacher, Mr. Maxwell, and other teachers in the school as Mr. Maxwell relieved them. Giving children opportunities to participate in different groupings with different teachers helped to solve the problems of the educationally handicapped at Pershing. Although they were intensively involved with several teachers, the children never lost the feeling that they belonged to one class; at the same time, they received the special assistance they needed.

The second extra teacher at Pershing, the remedial-reading teacher Glenda Gardner, follows the procedures pioneered by Mr. Maxwell. She, however, limits her assistance to reading whereas he works in every subject.

Although the program implemented by Mr. Maxwell and the remedial-reading teacher involves many students other than the educationally handicapped and poor readers, the total program at Pershing goes far beyond this one approach. Three other programs that expand educational opportunities augment the program financed by the funds for the educationally handicapped. Grades are not given in these three programs, nor is homework compulsory.

First let us examine what Mr. O'Donnell describes as "strength teaching." Each school year every teacher is encouraged to offer to teach a special skill or special interest that she may have. The principal and the district consultants are also encouraged to offer a special skill to the school. At Pershing, three parents also participate. The subjects offered in 1966 were:

Math
Number Line Slide Rule

Science
Rock Collections
Slides of the Southwest
Lapidary
Large-Scale Models

Language
Pantomime
Creative Writing
Flannel-Board Stories
Choral Speaking
Book Making
Role Playing
Spanish
German

Art
Water Colors
Egg-Shell Mosaics
Papier Mâché
  Animals
Batik
Crepe-Paper Flowers
Imaginary Characters

Art
Chalk Stencils
Ceramic Animals
Paper Sculpture
Crayon Techniques
Puppets—Paper Bag and Felt
Cut-Paper Art
Tissue-Paper Flowers
Toothpick Pictures
Gadget Printing
Sponge—Water Color
Scribble Art
Ceramics
Crewel Embroidery
Charcoal Drawing

Music
Song Bells
Spanish Songs
Vocal Music
Unison Singing

Physical Education
Gymnastics
Folk Dancing
Games

From the list of subjects, each teacher selects one for that semester and asks the teacher offering the subject to come to her class to teach it to her students. The requesting teacher remains with her class. Her presence maintains discipline, allows her to enjoy the experience along with her class, and allows her to see something that teachers rarely see: another teacher teaching *her* children and their reactions to the new teacher. There is little pressure on either the requesting teacher or the strength teacher because special skills are being offered; the strength teacher knows her subject and does not worry about doing poorly in front of another teacher. The class of the strength teacher is taken by the principal or by one of the two extra teachers in the school. They use a lesson plan prepared by the teacher.

Strength teaching is done every afternoon for six to eight weeks in the fall. Both students and teachers participate with enthusiasm. Teachers enjoy working with students either younger or older than their regular class. Teachers also like the program because they look at it as pure education; neither students nor teachers are evaluated. The opportunity to teach an interest to a class other than one's own is the major motivation to the strength teacher. Administration of the strength teaching program is the responsibility of a teacher volunteer, not the principal. Teachers interested in going into administration are available on every faculty. From the wide range of subjects taught by the strength teachers, one can see that the educational opportunities at the Pershing School far exceed those of the ordinary school curriculum.

In another program, teachers at Pershing conduct seminars for small groups of students selected for their ability. As many students as possible are chosen to participate. Students from different grades may be in the same seminar; that is, of eleven students in a seminar, some might be from fourth, some from fifth, and some from sixth grade. Students are encouraged to explore subjects of interest that are new to them. To quote Mr. O'Donnell, "The emphasis is not on measurable knowledge gained, but rather on the learning experience." For example, in one seminar, the Study of Culture, the students decided to create a civilization. Grappling with all the problems of overpopulation, overcrowding, and urban living, they discussed the means of creating an ideal society.

In the seminars, the students, together with the teacher who volunteers to lead the group, select the subject to be discussed.

Held twice a week for 45 minutes throughout the school year, the seminars encourage free expression and interchange. Because the teacher and students become deeply involved with each other, the students' motivation to learn is enhanced. Again, the principal and extra teachers take the classes of the seminar teachers while they are leading the seminars. Seminars may be held in the principal's office or the library, in the cafeteria or the patios, on playing field or lawn; the place is far less important than the ideas discussed. As shown in the table below, which covers a year at the Pershing School, the seminars are divided between primary and intermediate grades.

K–3	Study of culture	Art-inquiry training	New mathematical ideas	Creative arts and crafts	Spanish
4–6	Scientific discovery	Literature	Speech and drama	Music appreciation	Advanced math

In addition to the seminars and the special-assistance teaching, which continue for the entire year, and the strength teaching, which takes place in the fall, there is an enrichment program that begins in the spring and continues to the end of school. Mr. O'Donnell believes that, because students get tired toward the end of the school year even in the best school, a special enrichment program will motivate teachers and students to end the school year on a high note. The enrichment program is offered to older students, grades three to six, twice a week for one hour at the end of the school day. Whereas the strength teaching and, to some extent, the seminars reflect the choice and the skills of the teachers, the enrichment program is designed to reflect the choice and the skills of the students. The enrichment program is planned by the Student Council, which polls each child in the school asking him to give three choices of activities he would like to participate in or subjects he would like to learn. The Student Council sorts the students' requests and assigns groups of students to teachers who attempt to fulfill the specific requests of each group. So that there will be enough teachers, the primary teachers, who ordinarily would go home at 2:30 on these days, are asked to stay for an extra hour to teach in the enrichment program. Because of the students' great interest in the program, there is no difficulty persuading the primary teachers to stay two hours more a week for the last nine weeks of the school year. By using the primary teachers, the regular teachers, the principal and, in the case of the Pershing School, the janitor, who teaches trampoline gymnastics, it has been possible to give 85 percent of the students their first choice. Students who don't get their first choice are usually well-satisfied with their second or third choice.

The enrichment program offered in 1966–67 is shown below.

Students with consistent academic achievement				
Creative Writing	Math	Library Reading	Creative Expression	Literature
3–4	3–4	5–6	5–6	5–6
Students with high interest in specific field				
Nature Study	Around the World	Fundamentals of Architecture	Life in a Drop of Water	Public Speaking
3–4	3–4	4–5–6	5–6	5–6
Activity-centered programs				
Music	Drama	Arts and Crafts	Art Ideas	Drawing
3–4	3–4	3–4	5–6	5–6
Special areas				
Singing for fun	Oil Painting	Handwriting	Singing and Composing	
3–4	4–5–6	4–5–6	5–6	

Except for singing and drama, class size is reduced to twelve. Teachers have found the enrichment program to be an exciting experience; as in the other special programs, students have the opportunity to become involved with teachers they might ordinarily never get to know.

In the three imaginative programs at Pershing just described, the three cornerstones of education—involvement, relevance, and thinking—are a reality, not an ideal. Available to any school that wants to implement them, the programs have given the children an educational experience equaled by few public or private schools in America.

In the spring of 1968, the class meetings described in Chapters 10 through 12 were introduced into the Pershing School and became part of the regular teaching procedure in about 25 percent of the classes. As in other schools, the teachers who do not form the class into a circle and do not hold meetings regularly are having difficulty. Those who are succeeding are enthusiastic, but it should be noted that even in this excellent school and with firm administrative support, the class meetings are not being quickly or widely accepted by the teachers. Mr. O'Donnell predicts that half the teachers will be holding meetings by June, and he hopes for more next year. O'Donnell believes that, as good as his program is, the class discussions can add a new dimension, a belief shared by several teachers who have discovered their value.

At Pershing there is no educational tradition except involvement, relevance, and thinking. Any procedure which does not advance this tradition has no place in the school. Thoughtful change is the order of the day.

A final note to this chapter. With some reluctance but with great expectations, Mr. O'Donnell and two key members of his staff will leave the Pershing School in June, 1968, to form the nucleus of a new staff at an elementary school in Palo Alto, California. Combining our ideas, the three men from Pershing and I (acting as a consultant) will institute a program that we hope will become a model for elementary schools. This opportunity has been made possible by Dr. Harold Santee, the Superintendent of the Palo Alto Schools, who has long held beliefs similar to those expressed in this book and by Mr. O'Donnell, and who wants to translate what he believes into reality. With his help, we hope to make this school not only work for the children of Palo Alto, but also serve as a demonstration and training center for educators interested in observing our ideas in practice.

CHAPTER SIXTEEN

The Upper Grades

Although most of this book is applicable to education at any grade level, the examples and the detailed suggestions have been directed primarily toward the elementary school. My purpose for this emphasis has been clearly stated: without a good start, students have little chance to succeed in any secondary school. Children who don't read in elementary school find high school about the same regardless of program, teachers, or philosophy. But, of the children who leave elementary school with a fairly good foundation, many will fail in a secondary school that does not have a relevant, thoughtful, involved program.

Most high schools have a good academic program for students who are college-bound. In addition, some large central-city high schools have an adequate vocational program for those interested in a few specific vocations such as auto mechanics. Many students, however, who are neither college-bound nor vocationally set find little of either academic or vocational significance to keep them in school, and they drop out. To be realistic, however, the vocational training offered in large schools is often either obsolete or available to far fewer students than wish to enroll. Few high schools can afford to purchase or maintain the equipment necessary to keep current with the specialized knowledge demanded by modern technical jobs. Fortunately, most nonprofessional vocations actually require little specialized prevocational training; the necessary specific skills can be learned best on the job. The call is for responsible students who graduate from high school with the skills (mostly reading and arithmetic) to learn quickly. Many personnel men with whom I have talked stress that personal responsibility and basic skills are more important than specific skills learned in high school. A responsible trainee—one who comes to work on time, listens to instruction, and helps others—is more eagerly sought than the trainee with extensive vocational preparation but poor personal characteristics.

Whether or not the secondary schools really do a good job of preparing students for college or work, the public thinks they are more important and is willing to spend much more money on them than on the primary schools. *I contend that this priority is wrong, that primary school is more important, and that more money should be spent there getting children well started.* The high school should continue to teach skills and should integrate them into the knowledge courses. Every student should become competent in the communication skills—reading, writing, and speaking. Teaching of the arts—that is, giving students enough knowledge of and exposure to an art to enable them to enjoy it—should also receive greater emphasis in high schools. Many college students have so many required courses in their major subject that they cannot take courses in the arts and the humanities.

The suggestions made for making involvement, relevance, and thinking a reality in the schools will be more readily accepted by the elementary schools than by the high schools. The elected officials who control the policies of our schools usually agree that these three concepts are important for the elementary school student. High school teachers, however, who incorporate them into their teaching may be criticized or even fired. Relevance is particularly feared. Although we pride ourselves on our free society (at least in our speeches), we tend to distrust teachers who get too involved with older students and get them thinking about the relevant issues of our times. We never learn that we must become involved with students in discussing relevant subjects when they are young, when they trust us and look up to us. Our failure to do so is a major cause of the mistrust so prevalent today. For example, *the intellectual topics important to adults reading this book (such as the war, politics, religion, abortion, love, sex, pills, family planning, zoning, lobbying, taxes, and the draft) are never discussed in depth and with meaning in any school.* If I am wrong, I am willing to stand corrected, but I know that few, if any, teachers or students can effectively refute this statement.

The ideas, especially about relevance, that I present in this chapter will anger some and dismay others. Many will dismiss my ideas as praiseworthy but impractical. Unfortunately, unless we try some of the so-called impractical ideas, we will find that more and more students fail; failure is the most impractical result of education. We can only tolerate a certain percentage of failure before we get social disorganization. I don't know what this percentage is, but I know it is already past the critical point in much of our central-city areas and it is increasing in suburbia.

Several years ago I was invited to act as chairman of a student panel that was part of a PTA program at the elementary school my children attend. Seven tenth-grade students who had entered the school when it opened ten years before had been invited back to discuss their elementary school experience as it related to junior and now senior high. Thoughtful and generally successful, the students came from homes in which education is stressed. The discussion centered on how different the impersonal junior and senior high schools were from their recollection of a more personal elementary school. Although in reality elementary school was not particularly personal or involving, in retrospect it seemed so in comparison with their present school. The difference was very important to them. They believed that the elementary school did not prepare them well for the shock of impersonal secondary education. Eliminating this shock, of course, is not the problem of the elementary school; the changes obviously need to be made in the secondary schools. Repeatedly complaining that in junior or senior high they didn't get to know the teachers very well, the students said that they therefore often had trouble figuring out what was expected of them. Now they were just faces in assigned seats rather than the well known Jim, Jan, or Joan of their first six years of school. Resigned to not getting to know their teachers well, they were not happy about it. Again and again they asked, "Is there some way we can get to know our teachers better and some way our teachers can get to know us better?" These students were uninvolved and bitterly complaining.

The second major point that these successful students made was that their education had little relationship to their lives. Curiously enough, they accepted this much more willingly than the lack of involvement. There is so little relevance to much of their school work that they had not had enough experience with relevant education even to know what they were missing. Not really expecting school to relate to their lives, the students thought they could learn enough about the world in the intellectual atmosphere of their education-conscious homes; the lack of involvement and the increasing anonymity of school, however, were overwhelming. Being closely involved with their parents and other adults in the community and having been close to their teachers in elementary school, they resented their inability to get close to their teachers in junior and senior high.

Children without high internal and external motivation feel the pain of impersonal secondary education more acutely than children with greater motivation. It is my belief, confirmed by years of talking to the girls at Ventura, that children with low motivation feel so much pain that they withdraw from school either physically or mentally. Giving up trying to become involved, they accept school as an impersonal place that does not contribute to fulfilling their needs. The motivated students react to the pain by trying harder; the others get rid of the pain by failing and dropping out.

In addition to eliminating the bad educational practices described in earlier chapters, we should work toward making high school a warmer, more personal place for the student. This is not coddling the students; on the contrary, it is both simple humanity and common sense—the former because we reduce or eliminate the pain felt by the students, the latter because we make education better without spending any more money. If we do spend more money on the schools, as some people believe is necessary, we will gain little benefit from it unless we create an environment of greater involvement.

Solving the problem of impersonality in secondary schools is not easy. One suggestion that I believe has merit is to increase the use of the home room. Ordinarily used only for clerical procedures and announcements, the home room can, given more time, also be used for social-problem-solving and open-ended class meetings similar to those for elementary students described in Chapter 10. Held once or twice a week, the meetings can be a major step toward reducing the impersonality of the secondary schools. In addition, class meetings can be held in social studies and perhaps other classes at least once a week. In the class meetings, the students and teachers will get to know each other better. Students become involved with teachers in a problem-solving experience in which no one can fail. To allow time for the class meetings, some less important courses may have to be dropped from the curriculum.

Students experienced in class meetings will be better able to participate in whole-class discussions of the regular subject material. We can't teach students as individuals when we have large classes. Class discussions should be used more extensively; they provide opportunity for both individual participation and group involvement.

Impersonality in high school can also be reduced by allowing all students to participate in the extracurricular activities. Beginning in elementary school and culminating in high school, the most desirable and enjoyable activities are available only to the most talented, the most skilled, or the most intelligent and hard-working. The average athlete, the average scholar, the average actor, the average musician is usually left out. As discussed in Chapter 6, even talented students often cannot participate unless they have good grades. At the Ventura School we try to ensure that the extracurricular activities (and ours are most limited) are not dominated by a few; public schools can do the same. The Pershing School is an example at the elementary level of a program that involves all the students. Similar programs can be developed and used in the junior and senior high. For talented students with good grades (that is, those who are allowed to participate), involvement in extracurricular activities somewhat makes up for the lack of involvement they have in regular classes. But it is the average and below-average student, even more than the successful one, who needs the personal contact with the faculty inherent in these activities. Association with the better and more talented students increases his chance for success. Because success in extracurricular activities (as well as in the academic program) is so highly related to involvement, we must try to get every student involved. Sharply separating the successes, who get whatever is good in the school, from the failures, who get next to nothing, the present system can be changed only by ensuring that the two groups associate through giving the failure group an opportunity to participate in athletics, music, drama, and other interesting activities of the school.

A serious problem in the secondary school is the student who does badly and who seems to have little motivation to do better. Many teachers say that if they had more time to work individually with these students, they could teach them much more. Unfortunately, the large classes in most high schools prevent

teachers from giving students much individual attention. One
way to make up for the lack of teacher time is for more able
students to help those doing badly in particular subjects. Such a
program has been implemented successfully in several schools.
The tutors can volunteer, or perhaps be assigned by the teacher.
Student tutors have the time, as teachers do not, to give significant help to their slower schoolmates. In the upper grades, the
student tutors would necessarily be from approximately the
same grade level; in the lower grades, older tutors seem to help
the most. Much of the success of the tutoring program is
probably due to the association and personal attention that the
successful student gives to the failing student. Failing students
ordinarily associate only with each other and never know the
successful ones. During the tutoring session, students of varying
abilities are together in a situation that benefits both. In addition to helping the slow student, the tutor himself learns more
about the subject as he tries to make it understandable to his
pupil.

Studies of student tutoring have also shown, somewhat surprisingly, that, given the opportunity and given encouragement, failing students can be used to tutor younger failing
students successfully. Apparently the student who does poorly,
when asked to help another student, begins to identify not as a
failure but as a success; as a success he works to correct the
deficiencies in his own education so that he can become an
effective tutor. The student he is working with senses that, although his tutor has been a failure, he no longer has the attitude of a failure, and has gained the motivation to learn. Seeing
the change gives the poor student motivation to change also. At
Ventura, I have often observed this phenomenon. Bright and
interested girls who had previously done poorly in school tutored successfully; sometimes they were even able to teach il-
literate girls to read.

At present student tutors are rarely used; when they are, it is
usually within one school or in adjacent schools. Current tutor-

ing programs using college students and adults, under VISTA and other programs, are good but too limited. The most effective implementation will come from using the student body itself.

A constant complaint of students is that their schoolwork doesn't prepare them for living in the real world; it seems to be something apart from and distinct from life. The students' complaint is justified partly because the schools are isolated from the rest of the community. To break down this isolation, the schools must find people in the community willing to talk to students in both large and small groups. Chosen from every occupation, they should be articulate, warm, and personal. Responsible community leaders should be asked to come to school, not to give a formal speech or to exhort students to study harder, but to talk warmly, personally, and, above all, *honestly with* (not *to*) groups of interested students. Students complain, with some justification, that the adult world talks down to them. More accurately, perhaps, adults fail altogether to make contact with adolescents. We expect that somehow or other our failure to talk to and to listen to each other will eventually disappear. When it does not, we accept fatalistically our inability to communicate, as has each generation before us since the time of Socrates.

One of the reasons that the widely publicized generation gap persists is that the responsible adults in the community talk to each other about the students instead of talking with the students about their common world. Talking with students can help make what they learn in school alive; otherwise, it's mostly just dead knowledge. A judge, for example, can talk to students about his feelings about the young people he finds in front of him in court, his concern about why they are there, and his thoughts on how they might have done better. His talk, an honest appraisal of his position in the community with respect to adolescents, can include answering questions by the students. After conversations such as this with judges, and similar ones with policemen, students will more likely maintain respect for the law. Ministers, lawyers, doctors, and politicians can also be asked to come to school and honestly exchange ideas with students. It is the responsibility of people in all walks of life, public and private, to talk with students, to encourage students to ask questions, and, if necessary, to return to answer these questions. If they respect our young citizens, they, in turn, will gain their respect. School administrators and school boards should not only be strong enough to permit these exchanges, they should be the leaders in bringing them about.

Equally important to having responsible adults talk with students in school is giving students the chance to express their ideas to the adults who have control over their lives in school. In most meetings of school boards, faculties, and parents with teachers, students should be included and asked for their opinions. Our failure to maintain a dialogue with students sows the seeds for our current campus disruptions, which are attempts by students to get adults to listen. We can bounce signals off the moon, but we haven't learned to communicate with our young people. Can our failure to do so mean that as adults we are afraid to hear what the younger generation has to say because it may be closer to the truth than our own rationalizations? The class meeting on lying described in Chapter 13 indicates that the answer is yes. We need to see ourselves as young people see us. We must listen and talk to them, and so must the schools and the community. An isolated school is an irrelevant school.

Another way for the school to maintain contact with the community is to invite back its graduates, both successful and failing. When a girl returns to the Ventura School to visit after having been gone for some time, both her old friends and the newer girls are eager to talk to her to find out what she is doing, where she is having problems, and where she is succeeding. We could lecture for a year and not help as much as one girl returning to the school who has a successful job, is successful in school, or is successfully married. Visits with graduates can be of equal value in high school. Graduates of one to ten years are of the same generation as the students, so communication is intact, yet they have had experience that the students have not. Graduates should be invited back to discuss with students not only their successes, but their failures. The discussion should center on their lives since leaving school and how they relate their education to what has happened to them. The opinions of young graduates could also be valuable to school officials. They have been out of school long enough to have gained some perspective, but not so long that the schools are not reasonably the same or that they have forgotten what it was really like.

As in the elementary school, discipline is important in the secondary school. After some of the suggestions of this book are put into practice, disciplinary problems will decrease, as they did at the Ventura School. When education is involved, relevant, and thoughtful, students succeed and there is less turmoil. But there will always be problems. In Chapter 14 I stressed that good education cannot take place in a chaotic atmosphere. The students should have a voice in making rules and in changing them, but no excuse is acceptable for not following reasonable rules. Some students, however, will not follow the rules, and the school must deal with them in a positive way. As I have said, punishment does not work; students who break the rules in high school have been punished so often it means nothing to them. Although there are more counselors in high school than in elementary school, there are not enough for individual counseling. In any case, my experience has shown that group counseling is almost always more effective than individual counseling, and that groups of ten to twenty are more effective than groups of five to ten.

Treating the unsuccessful students in a group by themselves, however, is usually ineffective. Needing involvement with successful students to become successful themselves, they should be intermixed with successful students. Successful students can be asked, or required, to join groups in which the school failures attempt to solve their problems. Because no one is completely successful and no one is a complete failure, in a mixed group each student can both help and learn from every other student. Most students will enjoy the group meetings, and certainly no one will be harmed. Even in Ventura we found that we needed to mix our girls at random so that the strongest and the most motivated could help us with the weakest girls. Groups containing only irresponsible girls had little success. Led by counselors, teachers, or administrators, the groups can meet after school or, at least for the first few meetings, during school hours. Punishment of students should never come from the meetings (or from any other school procedure). Suspension should be used as a last resort. Recalcitrant students should go from the group to suspension when they are totally uncooperative, and from suspension to the group when they choose to try again. Although group meetings should of course discuss student problems, they should also be led into open-ended intellectual discussions so that the failing students can think and gain the pleasure of doing so in the company of other thinking students. They often surprise themselves. As I discussed in Chapter 11, meetings continually harping on a disciplinary problem aren't as effective as involved, interesting group discussions on intellectual subjects. Interesting discussions build involvement; disciplinary problems are fewer as involvement becomes stronger. High schools should use these groups as the major disciplinary procedure. Minor discipline can be handled in the home-room meetings; the special groups should be reserved for major rule infractions and consistent failures.

A good way to motivate students who have had bad records is to give them recognition when they start doing well. Many schools use bad conduct or deficiency reports; few schools send special notes home telling parents about good conduct or good scholarship. Available in every system, these notes should be used much more frequently than they are at present. Rather than give a student a bad-conduct report, handle the problem in school. When his behavior improves, send a good-conduct note to his parents. By giving the student recognition for his improvement, the note may decrease friction between him and his parents.

Few meetings should be held with parents about serious disciplinary problems. Bringing to school the parents of a child who is causing problems often does more harm than good. Becoming anxious and upset, the parents blame the child for causing them discomfort. They usually punish the child, making the situation worse instead of better. If parents are called in, the student should always be present when he is discussed. The administrator or counselor should immediately set the stage for a constructive solution by saying, "We are not trying to find out whose fault the problem is; we are looking for a way to solve it." Student and parent participation should be limited to constructive suggestions, not, as is too often the case, to fault finding and recrimination. The recommendations should be brief and understandable to everyone. After they have been agreed upon, they should be put in writing and the student should commit himself in writing to following them. To repeat, however, parents should be brought to school only after all efforts by the school to work with the student alone have failed. Students do not learn maturity and responsibility by having their parents called in; they learn it by dealing with problems where they exist, in school, with school people.

Nothing provokes more anxiety in the secondary school than grades and tests. In Chapter 8 I recommended that A-B-C-D-F grading be replaced by the pass-superior system, and in Chapter 7 I recommended that objective tests not be used for evaluation. Here I shall offer a specific suggestion about examinations, a suggestion that I believe can help make education a true intellectual effort, reduce student anxiety, and make any grading system better. At present, students are given little responsibility in evaluating what is important or not important in their courses. Blindly accepting the teacher's judgment, the students try to discover what he considers most important. There is nothing wrong with teachers telling students what they think is most important. But there is also nothing wrong with the students criticizing the teacher's opinions and giving their own ideas about the course.

A suggestion I have made to some college teachers that a few of them have tried and found to work well is to make students responsible for their own tests. The students can be asked to submit weekly one or several discussion questions relevant to the material studied that week. (This suggestion does not apply to courses, such as mathematics, in which problem solving is the main educational tool.) The teacher evaluates the questions either during class or by written comments. After the student revises the questions, he hands them back. At the end of the semester, the teacher selects some of the questions to be used as the student's final examination. The teacher's evaluation of the student in the course is based on (1) the questions the student asked, and (2) his ability at the end of the semester to give thoughtful answers to his own questions. Each student receives his own questions; students are not responsible for answering questions presented by other students. Certainly no student can complain that the teacher gave an unfair examination. The teacher's job is to present the course so that the students could ask and answer sensible questions. Any student who can do so has learned the subject. If the teacher cannot get students to ask important, relevant questions, he should examine his teaching, not just question the student's ability to learn.

The suggestions of this chapter, if put into practice, will correct some of the present defects of secondary education. Necessarily coupled with the suggestions made for the elementary school, they would be applied to students who had graduated from elementary school with a background of involvement and problem solving and who were now ready for a junior or senior high school with the same orientation. I do not claim that these ideas are the answer to all the problems of the secondary school.

My limited experience in secondary schools has prevented me from analyzing the contents of courses. It is clear, however, that irrelevance and undue emphasis on facts lead to many student problems. I hope that educators who agree with the ideas of this book will work to improve course content. But unless we greatly improve primary schools, especially in the central city, what happens in the secondary schools will be academic. I have emphasized the primary schools because it is far easier to prevent problems than to patch failures. If this book helps to prevent failure, it has served its purpose.

I have offered some suggestions that I hope will help to return education to its original purpose: to produce a thoughtful, creative, emotionally alive, unafraid man, a man willing to try to solve the problems he faces in his world. Although he may not solve all of them, he will solve some of them. Confident that he can build on his success, he may fail for a while, but he will know that some success is possible. And when success does not come easily, he will not give up. If he can think, if he can relate to his fellow man, if he can appreciate the beauty created by man and nature, he has a chance for happiness and a chance to feel worthwhile. Education can do no more for a man. The rest is up to him.

INDEX

Health, 185
Heffernan, Helen, 33n.
Heterogeneous classes, 98–99, 206
    academic reasons for, 89–94
    advantages of, 81–89
    and prevention of failure, 81–94
High schools, 81, 103–108, 215–228
    grading in, 103–108, 226–227
    impersonality in, 219–220
Hippies, 174–175
Home rooms, 219
Homes, broken, 3, 5
    and homework, 75
    middle-class, 49–50
    upper-class, 50–52
    See also Family life; Parents
Homework, 72–75
    parents and, 170
Homogeneous reading classes, 88–89,
    91–93, 115
Human relations, 2, 4, 6–17, 42, 183

Ideas, 53, 77
    expression of, 52, 223
    new, teacher's attitude toward, 114–
    116
    See also Opinions
Identity, 24–25
    success, 13–17, 41–42
Imagination, 175–178
Incorrigibility, 2
    See also Behavior
Involvement, 19–21, 23–24, 213–214,
    216, 224–225, 227
    teacher-pupil, 219
I.Q., 84
Issues, understanding of, 77

Jacobson, Lenore, 82n.
James, H. Thomas, quoted, 112
Jargon, 70

Katz, Joseph, 44
Kaufman, Bel, 57

Kindergarten, 25, 28–29, 31, 101, 165,
    171
Knowledge, skills versus, 89
Krider, Mary A., and Mary Petsche,
    28n.

Leadership, 154
Learning, grades and, 61, 65
    related to life, 50, 52–53
    See also Relevance
Leisure, 180–181
Loneliness, failure and, 16–18
Los Angeles, 4, 9, 45, 121, 155, 157
Love, 14–15, 172–173
    need for, 12–13
    as social responsibility, 14
Lying, 161, 187–191

Marriage, 3, 5, 182–183
Mathematics, 55–56, 69, 89–91, 183–
    184
Maxwell, Keith, 206–209
Melrose School, 65–67, 80
Memorizing, 29–30, 81
    tests and, 70, 72
    thinking versus, 33–44
Mental illness, 16, 19
Mexican Americans, 10, 198
Miramonte School, 155
Money, 184
Morality, 186–192
Motivation, 18–19, 39–40
    lack of, 11, 18, 220
    to learn, 49
Mount St. Mary's College, 121
Movies, 57–58

Needs, fulfillment of, 16, 19
    for love, 12–13
    for self-worth, 12–13
Negroes, 10, 50, 198
Normal curve, 70–72

Oak School, 82–83
O'Donnell, Donald, 204–206, 208, 210–
    212, 214

ABOUT THE AUTHOR

William Glasser was born in 1925 in Cleveland, Ohio, where
he attended Cleveland Heights High School, Case Institute of
Technology, and Western Reserve University School of Medicine. A chemical engineer at nineteen, he became a clinical
psychologist at twenty-three and a physician at twenty-eight.
After medical school he received his psychiatric training at the
Veterans Administration Center and UCLA.

Dr. Glasser has been a psychiatrist in private practice in Los
Angeles since 1957 and has consulted widely in the correctional
field. His method of treating juvenile delinquents has gained
wide recognition. He was for some years the regular consultant
at the Ventura School for Girls of the California Youth Authority and the Los Angeles Orthopaedic Hospital.

Recently he has devoted himself more and more to education at various levels. He has taught a large group of city and
county school administrators, counselors, and teachers. He has
worked directly with children in the Los Angeles City schools—
Watts and other areas—and the Palo Alto schools. He has lec-
tured widely in this country and Canada about the problems of
contemporary education.

In order to help more people understand his ideas about
education he has recently been able to establish, through the
generosity of the Stone Foundation, the Educator Training
Center, 2140 Olympic Boulevard, Los Angeles, California 90006.

71 72 73 74   12 11